All About Atlantic Ocean: A Kid's Guide to Its Amazing Features

Educational Books For Kids, Volume 35

Shah Rukh

Published by Shah Rukh, 2024.

While every precaution has been taken in the preparation of this book, the publisher assumes no responsibility for errors or omissions, or for damages resulting from the use of the information contained herein.

ALL ABOUT ATLANTIC OCEAN: A KID'S GUIDE TO ITS AMAZING FEATURES

First edition. October 22, 2024.

Copyright © 2024 Shah Rukh.

ISBN: 979-8227624482

Written by Shah Rukh.

Table of Contents

Prologue...1
Chapter 1: The Mighty Waves of the Atlantic......................................2
Chapter 2: Exploring the Deepest Part of the Ocean...........................6
Chapter 3: The Atlantic's Famous Ocean Currents 11
Chapter 4: The Mysterious Bermuda Triangle 16
Chapter 5: The Great Atlantic Ocean Tides.......................................21
Chapter 6: Discovering the Gulf Stream 26
Chapter 7: Sea Life of the Atlantic Ocean 31
Chapter 8: The History of Atlantic Shipwrecks 36
Chapter 9: How Islands Form in the Atlantic...................................40
Chapter 10: Atlantic Hurricanes and Storms 45
Chapter 11: The Underwater Mountains and Ridges 50
Chapter 12: Exploring the Cold Waters of the North Atlantic....55
Chapter 13: The Role of the Atlantic in World Exploration..........60
Chapter 14: The Atlantic Ocean's Coral Reefs 65
Chapter 15: Protecting the Atlantic from Pollution.......................70
Chapter 16: Amazing Facts About Atlantic Waves..........................75
Chapter 17: Ancient Legends of the Atlantic Ocean 80
Chapter 18: Atlantic Ocean's Impact on Global Climate.............85
Chapter 19: The Trade Routes of the Atlantic 90
Chapter 20: Life Along the Atlantic Coastlines 95
Epilogue.. 100

Prologue

Welcome to an exciting journey across the vast and mysterious Atlantic Ocean! Have you ever wondered what secrets lie beneath its waves or how its waters have shaped the world we live in? The Atlantic Ocean is not just a huge body of water—it's home to incredible sea creatures, powerful currents, ancient shipwrecks, and stories that have been told for centuries. From the mysterious Bermuda Triangle to the busy trade routes that connect continents, the Atlantic has played a big role in history, science, and adventure.

In this book, you're going to dive deep (and sometimes stay close to shore) as we explore the amazing features of the Atlantic Ocean. You'll learn how islands form, discover what makes ocean tides so strong, and even uncover the legends that surround its waters. Whether you're fascinated by sharks, curious about underwater mountains, or eager to learn about hurricanes, there's something in the Atlantic Ocean for everyone!

So, grab your imaginary snorkel, put on your explorer's hat, and get ready to sail through the wonders of one of the world's greatest oceans. Let's dive in!

Chapter 1: The Mighty Waves of the Atlantic

The mighty waves of the Atlantic Ocean are a fascinating and powerful force of nature. Imagine standing on the beach, feeling the cool breeze on your face, and watching the waves rolling in from far away. These waves can be small and gentle, perfect for splashing around, but they can also grow enormous, towering as high as buildings! The Atlantic Ocean is known for having some of the biggest and most exciting waves in the world, and these waves are created by different forces working together.

First, let's think about where waves come from. Waves don't just appear out of nowhere. They start their journey far out in the middle of the ocean, sometimes thousands of miles away from the shore. One of the main causes of waves is the wind. When the wind blows across the surface of the ocean, it pushes the water, creating ripples that eventually grow into waves. The stronger and longer the wind blows, the bigger the waves can become. In the Atlantic Ocean, there are areas where the wind blows very hard and for long periods, which helps create massive waves.

But it's not just the wind that makes waves. Waves can also be created by underwater earthquakes or volcanic eruptions. When something like that happens, it causes the water to move suddenly, and that movement can create huge waves known as tsunamis. Although tsunamis are rare, they are extremely powerful and can travel across the entire Atlantic Ocean at incredible speeds. Even though most waves in the Atlantic are not caused by earthquakes, it's still amazing to think about how forces deep beneath the ocean can affect the water above.

The Atlantic Ocean is also special because of its vast size. It's the second-largest ocean in the world, and its size means that waves have plenty of space to grow as they travel across the water. The distance that a wave travels is called its "fetch," and in the Atlantic, the fetch can be very long. The longer the fetch, the bigger the waves can become. For example, waves that start near the coast of Africa can travel all the way across the ocean to the shores of the Americas. By the time they reach land, they've had time to grow larger and stronger.

The waves in the Atlantic are also affected by the shape of the ocean floor. The bottom of the ocean isn't flat; it's full of mountains, valleys, and deep trenches. As waves move across the ocean, they interact with these underwater features, which can cause them to change shape or even become more powerful. When waves get closer to shore, the ocean becomes shallower, and the waves start to slow down. This causes the top of the wave to rise up and eventually crash down onto the beach. That's why the waves you see at the beach are often bigger and more dramatic than the waves far out in the open ocean.

One of the most exciting places to see huge waves is off the coast of Portugal, at a spot called Nazaré. Here, the waves can grow to be as tall as 100 feet! These monster waves attract surfers from all over the world who come to ride them. Nazaré's waves are so big because of an underwater canyon that helps funnel the ocean's energy toward the shore, making the waves even more powerful. It's like nature's perfect playground for giant waves.

Waves aren't just fun for surfers, though. They play an important role in shaping the coastline. Over time, waves crashing against the shore can wear away rocks and cliffs, creating new landscapes. This process is called erosion, and it's been happening for millions of years. Some of the world's most beautiful beaches and coastlines have been shaped by the constant movement of waves. The Atlantic's waves have created everything from sandy shores to dramatic cliffs that rise high above the water.

Waves also help the ocean by mixing the water. As they move, waves stir up the surface of the ocean, bringing nutrients from the deep up to the top where they can be used by marine life. This mixing is important for tiny organisms called plankton, which are the base of the ocean food chain. Without waves, the ocean wouldn't be as healthy or as full of life. The constant movement of waves also helps the ocean absorb gases from the air, like oxygen, which fish and other sea creatures need to breathe.

Another amazing thing about waves is that they never really stop. Even on the calmest days, when the ocean looks flat and still, there are always tiny waves moving through the water. These small waves are called swells, and they are the leftover energy from winds that blew across the ocean days or even weeks earlier. Swells can travel long distances across the ocean, and when they finally reach the shore, they create gentle, rolling waves. Even when the weather is calm, the ocean is always in motion, and waves are constantly being created and moving through the water.

Sometimes, waves can become dangerous, especially during storms. The Atlantic Ocean is home to some of the most powerful storms on the planet, including hurricanes. Hurricanes are massive storms with strong winds that can create huge, dangerous waves. These waves can cause flooding and damage to coastal areas. During a hurricane, the ocean can become wild and unpredictable, with waves crashing violently against the shore. That's why people are often warned to stay away from the beach during storms, as the waves can be very powerful and unpredictable.

Despite their power, waves are also a source of wonder and beauty. People love to watch waves, whether they're sitting on the beach or out on a boat in the middle of the ocean. The sound of waves crashing against the shore can be calming, and the sight of waves rolling in can be mesmerizing. Waves are a reminder of the incredible energy and force of the ocean, and they show us just how connected our planet is, with winds, water, and even the moon working together to create these amazing natural wonders.

The mighty waves of the Atlantic Ocean are truly one of nature's most incredible features. They are constantly changing, moving, and shaping the world around them. Whether they are small ripples or towering giants, waves remind us of the power and beauty of the ocean. So, the next time you're at the beach, take a moment to watch the waves and think about the journey they've taken across the vast Atlantic. From gentle swells to massive breakers, every wave has a story to tell.

Chapter 2: Exploring the Deepest Part of the Ocean

Exploring the deepest part of the ocean is like taking a journey to a whole new world, one that is dark, mysterious, and filled with strange and wonderful creatures. The ocean is much deeper than most people imagine, and the deeper you go, the more incredible it becomes. At its deepest point, the ocean is nearly seven miles below the surface! That's deeper than Mount Everest is tall. This deepest part of the ocean is called the Mariana Trench, and within it lies the Challenger Deep, the very bottom of the trench and the deepest known point in the Earth's oceans.

The journey to the deepest part of the ocean begins at the surface, where the sunlight shines brightly, and the water is warm and full of life. Here, you'll find fish, dolphins, whales, and even coral reefs. But as you start to go deeper, things begin to change. The sunlight starts to fade, and the water becomes colder. At about 650 feet below the surface, there is no more light from the sun. This marks the beginning of the twilight zone, a place where only a little bit of light can reach. It's a spooky place where many animals glow in the dark to communicate, find food, or scare off predators. This glowing is called bioluminescence, and it's one of the most amazing adaptations in the ocean.

As you continue to travel deeper, past 3,300 feet, you enter the midnight zone. This part of the ocean is pitch black because no sunlight can reach here at all. The temperature drops to just above freezing, and the pressure becomes intense. Pressure is the weight of the water pushing down on everything, and at these depths, the pressure is thousands of times greater than what we feel at the surface. If humans tried to dive this deep without protection, they would be crushed by the weight of the water. That's why scientists who want to explore the deep ocean have to use special submarines or robotic vehicles that can withstand the immense pressure.

Even though it's so dark and cold, life still thrives in the midnight zone. Many of the creatures here are unlike anything you've ever seen before. Some have huge, sharp teeth, while others have glowing lures on their heads to attract prey. There are giant squid, strange jellyfish, and fish with bodies that seem almost transparent. The animals that live here have evolved to survive in this extreme environment, where food is scarce and the darkness never ends.

But the journey doesn't stop in the midnight zone. As we go even deeper, past 13,000 feet, we enter the abyssal zone, which covers much of the ocean floor. The water here is incredibly cold, and the pressure is even more crushing. The animals that live in the abyssal zone are often very slow-moving and have unique adaptations to help them survive in such harsh conditions. There are creatures like the abyssal octopus, which glides silently through the water, and the deep-sea anglerfish, which uses a glowing lure to catch its prey. The ocean floor in the abyssal zone is mostly flat and covered in thick layers of mud and sediment, but there are also underwater mountains and valleys that make this environment even more interesting.

Finally, we reach the hadal zone, which is named after Hades, the ancient Greek god of the underworld. This zone includes the deepest trenches in the ocean, such as the Mariana Trench. The hadal zone is the most extreme part of the ocean, with depths reaching over 36,000 feet. The pressure here is unimaginable—it's over 1,000 times greater than at the surface! Despite these extreme conditions, life still exists in the hadal zone. Some of the animals that live here are incredibly small, like tiny shrimp and worms, while others are larger, like the hadal snailfish, which has been found over 26,000 feet deep.

One of the most fascinating things about the deepest part of the ocean is how little we know about it. Even though humans have explored the surface of the moon and sent spacecraft to distant planets, we've only explored a small fraction of the ocean's depths. The deep ocean is like the last frontier on Earth, a place full of mysteries waiting to be discovered. Scientists are constantly sending new robotic submarines and advanced technology to explore these deep, dark places, and every time they do, they find something new.

For example, in 2012, filmmaker James Cameron made history by becoming the first person to dive solo to the bottom of the Mariana Trench in a specially designed submersible. His mission revealed amazing footage of the alien-like creatures living in the Challenger Deep. The walls of the trench were covered in strange organisms, and the floor was littered with unusual sea creatures. Cameron's expedition showed the world just how much there is to learn about the deep ocean and inspired new generations of explorers to keep searching for answers.

One of the reasons the deep ocean is so hard to explore is because of the intense pressure. As you go deeper, the pressure from the water above increases, and the deeper you go, the more pressure there is. At the bottom of the Mariana Trench, the pressure is about eight tons per square inch. That's like having 50 jumbo jets stacked on top of you! Because of this, scientists have to build very strong submarines that can withstand the pressure without being crushed.

Another challenge of exploring the deep ocean is the darkness. Since no sunlight reaches the deep ocean, explorers have to use powerful lights to see what's around them. Even then, the light only illuminates a small area, so it's easy to miss things. Many of the animals that live in the deep ocean are adapted to this darkness and use bioluminescence to communicate, find food, and avoid predators. Some animals, like the lanternfish, have special organs that produce light, while others, like the vampire squid, can create clouds of glowing mucus to confuse predators.

The cold temperatures in the deep ocean are also a challenge. As you descend deeper, the water becomes colder and colder, eventually reaching near-freezing temperatures. The animals that live in the deep ocean have special adaptations that allow them to survive in such cold conditions. Some deep-sea fish have antifreeze proteins in their blood to keep them from freezing, while other animals have slow metabolisms that help them conserve energy in the cold.

In addition to strange creatures and extreme conditions, the deep ocean is home to some of the most remarkable geological features on Earth. The ocean floor is covered with underwater mountains, deep valleys, and even hydrothermal vents, which are like underwater geysers that spew out superheated water full of minerals. These vents create a unique environment where strange creatures like giant tube worms and blind shrimp thrive, feeding on the chemicals released by the vents. Hydrothermal vents are one of the only places on Earth where life exists without sunlight, relying instead on chemical energy to survive.

The deepest part of the ocean is also a place where scientists believe life might have begun. Some scientists think that the extreme conditions around hydrothermal vents could have provided the perfect environment for the first forms of life to evolve billions of years ago. By studying the creatures that live in these deep, dark places, scientists hope to learn more about the origins of life on Earth and even the possibility of life on other planets.

As we continue to explore the deepest parts of the ocean, we're sure to make more incredible discoveries. The ocean is full of surprises, and every expedition brings new knowledge and understanding about our planet. The deep ocean is a reminder of just how vast and mysterious our world is, and it inspires us to keep exploring, learning, and discovering.

The deepest part of the ocean, with its towering trenches, fascinating creatures, and incredible geological formations, is truly one of the most amazing places on Earth. Even though it's dark, cold, and filled with challenges, it's also a place of wonder and beauty, where life has adapted to survive in ways that seem almost unbelievable.

Exploring the deepest part of the ocean is like unlocking the secrets of another world, and there's still so much more to discover.

Chapter 3: The Atlantic's Famous Ocean Currents

The Atlantic Ocean is like a giant water highway with some of the most famous ocean currents in the world. These currents are incredibly important because they help move water, heat, and nutrients all around the ocean, and they even affect the weather and climate of places far from the ocean. Imagine the Atlantic's currents as huge rivers that flow through the ocean, but unlike the rivers on land, these rivers don't have banks or borders—they move through the water, shaping life in the ocean and influencing life on land as well. One of the most well-known and powerful currents in the Atlantic is the Gulf Stream, but it's just one part of a much bigger system of currents that are constantly moving.

Ocean currents in the Atlantic are driven by several factors, including the rotation of the Earth, the wind, and differences in the temperature and saltiness of the water. These currents don't just stay at the surface—they flow deep down into the ocean as well. Some are warm, and others are cold, and together they create a complex network of water movement that stretches from the equator all the way to the polar regions.

The Gulf Stream is probably the most famous current in the Atlantic, and it's known for being a warm, fast-moving current. It starts in the Gulf of Mexico, flows up the east coast of the United States, and then crosses the Atlantic Ocean toward Europe. The Gulf Stream is like a giant conveyor belt, moving warm water from the tropics to the northern Atlantic. This warm water helps to keep places like Europe warmer than they would be otherwise. Even though Europe is much farther north than many places with similar climates, the warmth of the Gulf Stream keeps countries like the United Kingdom, Ireland, and Norway from being too cold in the winter. Without the Gulf Stream, these places would be much colder, with harsher winters, and the entire climate of Europe would be different.

The Gulf Stream doesn't just affect Europe's climate—it also plays a big role in the weather patterns on the east coast of North America. When the warm water of the Gulf Stream mixes with cold air coming from the Arctic, it can create powerful storms, including hurricanes. These storms can bring heavy rain, strong winds, and even flooding to coastal areas. In fact, the Gulf Stream is a major reason why the southeastern United States experiences so many hurricanes during the summer and fall. The warm waters of the Gulf Stream provide the energy that fuels these massive storms, making them stronger and more dangerous.

As the Gulf Stream moves across the Atlantic toward Europe, it splits into several smaller currents, including the North Atlantic Drift. This current continues to carry warm water northward, where it eventually meets colder waters near the Arctic. This is where something interesting happens—because the warm water of the Gulf Stream is saltier and denser than the cold water of the Arctic, it begins to sink. This sinking water is part of a process known as thermohaline circulation, which is a fancy way of saying that temperature and saltiness control the movement of water. When the warm, salty water of the Gulf Stream sinks, it creates a deep current that moves cold water back toward the equator. This deep current is like the return trip on the ocean's conveyor belt, and it plays a crucial role in balancing the Earth's climate.

Thermohaline circulation is sometimes called the "global conveyor belt" because it moves water all around the planet, not just in the Atlantic Ocean. It's a slow process—water can take hundreds or even thousands of years to complete the journey—but it's incredibly important. Without this global conveyor belt, the Earth's climate would be much less stable, and the oceans wouldn't be able to distribute heat and nutrients as effectively. In fact, scientists are studying the effects of climate change on the Atlantic's currents because there are concerns that global warming could slow down or even disrupt this system. If that happens, it could lead to big changes in weather patterns, sea levels, and marine life.

Another important current in the Atlantic is the Canary Current, which flows south along the west coast of Africa. Unlike the warm Gulf Stream, the Canary Current is a cold current, and it brings cooler water from the northern Atlantic down toward the equator. This current helps to keep the coastal regions of North Africa cooler than they might otherwise be, especially in places like Morocco. It also plays a big role in the process called upwelling. Upwelling happens when cold, nutrient-rich water from the deep ocean is brought up to the surface. This process is incredibly important for marine life because it brings nutrients that feed tiny organisms called plankton, which are the base of the food chain in the ocean. Plankton are eaten by small fish, which are then eaten by larger fish, and so on. Upwelling zones, like those created by the Canary Current, are some of the most productive areas in the ocean, meaning they are home to a huge number of fish and other sea creatures. Many fishing industries rely on these areas because they provide a steady supply of fish.

The Atlantic Ocean is also home to the Brazil Current, which flows southward along the coast of South America. This is a warm current, similar to the Gulf Stream, and it plays a big role in the climate of countries like Brazil and Uruguay. The warm waters of the Brazil Current help to keep the coastal areas warm and influence rainfall patterns. The Brazil Current eventually meets the colder waters of the Falkland Current, which comes up from the Southern Ocean. When these two currents meet, they create a mixing zone where warm and cold waters collide. This can lead to the formation of storms and other weather patterns, and it also affects marine life in the region.

Speaking of the Falkland Current, this cold current is another important part of the Atlantic's system. It flows northward from the icy waters of the Southern Ocean, bringing cold, nutrient-rich water along the coast of Argentina. Like the Canary Current, the Falkland Current helps to create upwelling zones, where nutrients from the deep ocean are brought to the surface. These upwelling zones support rich ecosystems, and the waters off the coast of Argentina are home to many species of fish, seabirds, and marine mammals.

In addition to these major currents, the Atlantic Ocean also has smaller, more localized currents that play important roles in their regions. For example, the Labrador Current flows southward along the coast of Canada, bringing cold water from the Arctic down into the northern Atlantic. This current helps to cool the waters around Newfoundland and the northeastern United States, and it plays a role in the formation of sea ice in the winter. The cold waters of the Labrador Current also mix with the warmer waters of the Gulf Stream, creating an area known as the Grand Banks. The Grand Banks are famous for being one of the richest fishing grounds in the world, thanks to the nutrients brought in by the mixing of these two currents.

The Atlantic's currents don't just affect the ocean itself—they also have a big impact on the climate and weather patterns of the entire planet. For example, the Gulf Stream helps to keep Europe warmer, while the Brazil Current influences rainfall in South America. These currents are also connected to larger climate systems, like the El Niño and La Niña phenomena, which can cause changes in weather patterns around the world. During an El Niño event, for example, warm water builds up in the Pacific Ocean, which can affect the Atlantic's currents and lead to changes in temperature, rainfall, and even hurricane activity.

In the Atlantic, currents also help to move animals around. Many species of fish, turtles, and marine mammals use these currents to migrate long distances. For example, the leatherback sea turtle, which is one of the largest and most endangered species of turtle, uses the Gulf Stream to travel from its nesting grounds in the Caribbean to feeding grounds in the North Atlantic. Humpback whales also use the currents of the Atlantic to migrate between their breeding grounds in the tropics and their feeding grounds in colder, nutrient-rich waters.

Ocean currents in the Atlantic are essential to life on Earth, and scientists are still studying how these currents work and how they might be affected by climate change. As the planet warms, there are concerns that some of the Atlantic's major currents could slow down or even stop altogether. This could have serious consequences for the climate, sea levels, and marine ecosystems. For example, if the Gulf Stream were to slow down, Europe could become much colder, and the weather patterns in North America could become more extreme.

The Atlantic's famous ocean currents are more than just moving water—they are powerful forces that shape the world's climate, weather, and ecosystems. From the warm, fast-moving Gulf Stream to the cold, nutrient-rich Canary and Falkland Currents, these currents play a crucial role in making the Atlantic Ocean one of the most dynamic and important bodies of water on the planet. Whether they're helping to feed marine life, moving heat around the globe, or influencing the weather, the Atlantic's currents are an essential part of life on Earth, and their impact can be felt far beyond the ocean itself.

Chapter 4: The Mysterious Bermuda Triangle

The Bermuda Triangle is one of the most mysterious and talked-about places on Earth, and it has fascinated people for many years. Located in the Atlantic Ocean, the Bermuda Triangle forms a rough triangle between three points: Miami in the United States, Bermuda, and Puerto Rico. This area has gained a reputation because of the strange and unexplained disappearances of ships, airplanes, and even people. Some call it the "Devil's Triangle" because of the many odd events that have happened there, and it has become a place of legends, mystery, and wild theories.

One of the first recorded incidents that sparked the Bermuda Triangle mystery happened in 1945, when five U.S. Navy bombers known as Flight 19 disappeared while on a training mission. The planes, along with 14 crew members, vanished without a trace. To make things even more mysterious, the search plane that was sent to find them also disappeared. This event captured the public's imagination, and soon, other stories of strange disappearances in the Bermuda Triangle began to surface. Some of these incidents involve large cargo ships, military planes, private yachts, and even commercial flights that seemed to vanish without any warning or explanation. The fact that many of these vessels and aircraft were never found, and no distress signals were sent, added to the sense of mystery surrounding the area.

One of the most famous disappearances in the Bermuda Triangle is that of the USS Cyclops, a massive Navy ship that vanished in 1918. The Cyclops was carrying a full crew and a large cargo of manganese ore when it sailed into the Bermuda Triangle, never to be seen again. No wreckage was ever found, and no one knows what happened to the ship or its crew of 309 people. It remains one of the greatest unsolved mysteries in maritime history, and it's one of the reasons the Bermuda Triangle became so famous.

The mystery doesn't stop with just ships—planes have also disappeared. In 1948, a commercial flight known as the Star Tiger vanished while flying over the Bermuda Triangle on its way from England to Bermuda. The plane and its passengers simply disappeared from radar, and no wreckage was ever found. Just one year later, in 1949, another plane, the Star Ariel, disappeared in a similar way. Both of these incidents happened in good weather, and there were no distress calls or signs of trouble before the planes vanished. These disappearances baffled investigators, and to this day, no one knows exactly what happened to these planes.

So, what could be behind all these strange disappearances? Over the years, people have come up with many different theories, some scientific and others more fantastical. One of the more common explanations is that powerful natural forces are at play in the Bermuda Triangle. The area is known for sudden and violent storms, which can develop quickly and without much warning. These storms can create dangerous waves, strong winds, and lightning that could potentially sink ships or cause planes to crash. Waterspouts, which are like tornadoes over the water, are also common in the Bermuda Triangle and could contribute to ships disappearing.

Another natural explanation involves something called "rogue waves." Rogue waves are extremely large and unpredictable waves that can appear out of nowhere, reaching heights of 100 feet or more. These waves are so powerful that they could easily capsize large ships and make them disappear without a trace. Some scientists believe that rogue waves might be more common in the Bermuda Triangle than in other parts of the ocean, which could explain why so many ships have disappeared there.

The ocean floor in the Bermuda Triangle is also very unusual. It's full of deep trenches, underwater mountains, and vast fields of shifting sand. If a ship were to sink in this area, it could quickly be covered by sand or fall into one of the deep underwater valleys, making it nearly impossible to find. The strong ocean currents in the area could also carry wreckage far away from the original site, which would explain why so few pieces of the missing ships or planes have ever been recovered.

Another interesting theory involves methane gas bubbles. Deep beneath the ocean floor, there are large deposits of methane gas trapped in the form of ice. If these methane gas deposits were to suddenly erupt, they could release massive bubbles of gas into the water. These bubbles could reduce the density of the water, making it less able to support the weight of a ship, which could cause the ship to sink rapidly and without warning. Some scientists have suggested that these methane eruptions could be responsible for some of the disappearances in the Bermuda Triangle.

Of course, not all of the theories about the Bermuda Triangle are scientific. Some people believe that the area is home to supernatural forces or even extraterrestrial activity. One of the more popular theories is that the Bermuda Triangle is actually a portal to another dimension or a gateway to a parallel universe. According to this theory, ships and planes that enter the Bermuda Triangle are somehow transported to another time or place, which is why they are never found. While there's no scientific evidence to support this idea, it has captured the imagination of many people who enjoy thinking about the mysteries of the unknown.

Another popular idea is that the Bermuda Triangle is home to an ancient, advanced civilization, like the lost city of Atlantis. Some believe that Atlantis, with its advanced technology, could be responsible for the strange occurrences in the Triangle. According to this theory, the technology of Atlantis is still active beneath the ocean, causing ships and planes to disappear. This idea is more of a legend than a scientifically supported theory, but it's one of the many stories that have contributed to the Bermuda Triangle's mysterious reputation.

One of the more recent scientific theories involves a phenomenon called "electronic fog." According to this idea, certain atmospheric conditions in the Bermuda Triangle could create a thick, electrically charged fog that interferes with the navigation systems of ships and planes. Pilots and captains could become disoriented and lose their way, leading to crashes or other accidents. Some people who have traveled through the Bermuda Triangle have reported experiencing strange electrical malfunctions or seeing unusual clouds or fog, which has led some to believe that electronic fog could be a real danger in the area.

Despite all these theories, the truth about the Bermuda Triangle remains elusive. While many of the disappearances can be explained by natural causes like storms, rogue waves, and human error, there are still many cases that remain unexplained. Ships and planes have disappeared in calm weather, and some of the wreckage has never been found. These unsolved mysteries continue to fuel speculation about what really happens in the Bermuda Triangle.

Over the years, some people have argued that the Bermuda Triangle isn't actually more dangerous than any other part of the ocean. The Atlantic Ocean is a busy place, with many ships and planes passing through every day. Given the large number of vessels traveling through the area, it's possible that the Bermuda Triangle has more accidents simply because it's such a heavily trafficked region. In fact, some scientists believe that the Bermuda Triangle has gained its mysterious reputation simply because of its location—it's near busy shipping lanes, flight paths, and popular tourist destinations, which means that when something does go wrong, it gets a lot of attention.

The Bermuda Triangle may also be a victim of its own legend. Once the idea of the Bermuda Triangle became popular, every disappearance in the area seemed to add to the mystery, even if the cause was perfectly ordinary. Human error, mechanical problems, and bad weather are often responsible for accidents at sea and in the air, but when they happen in the Bermuda Triangle, they are often seen as part of the larger mystery. This has helped to keep the legend alive and has made the Bermuda Triangle one of the most famous unexplained phenomena in the world.

Despite all the stories and legends, it's important to remember that the Bermuda Triangle is not a place to be afraid of. Thousands of ships and planes pass through the area every year without any problems. In fact, it's a popular destination for tourists who want to visit the beautiful islands of Bermuda, Puerto Rico, and the Bahamas. Modern technology, like GPS and radar, has made navigation much safer, and many of the mysterious disappearances from the past might not happen today thanks to these advances.

In the end, the Bermuda Triangle remains one of the most intriguing and mysterious places on Earth. Whether the disappearances are caused by natural forces, human error, or something more mysterious, the legend of the Bermuda Triangle continues to capture the imagination of people all over the world. It's a place where science and mystery meet, and while we may never know the full truth about what happens in the Bermuda Triangle, the stories and theories will continue to fascinate and inspire those who are curious about the unknown.

Chapter 5: The Great Atlantic Ocean Tides

The tides of the Atlantic Ocean are one of the most fascinating and powerful natural phenomena on our planet. Every day, the ocean's water rises and falls in a rhythmic cycle, creating high tides and low tides along the coastlines of countries bordering the Atlantic. But what causes these tides? Why do they happen in such a regular pattern? And how do they affect the people and animals that live near the ocean? To understand the amazing tides of the Atlantic, we need to dive deep into the science behind them, the forces that create them, and the incredible impact they have on our world.

Tides are caused by the gravitational pull of the moon and the sun. The moon, being much closer to Earth than the sun, has the most influence over the tides. As the moon orbits around our planet, its gravity pulls on the water in the oceans, causing the water to bulge out toward the moon. This creates what we call a high tide. At the same time, on the opposite side of the Earth, another high tide occurs because the Earth itself is being pulled slightly toward the moon, leaving behind a bulge of water on the far side. So, at any given time, there are two high tides happening on Earth—one on the side facing the moon and one on the opposite side.

But it's not just the moon that affects the tides. The sun also plays a role, although its gravitational pull is weaker than the moon's because it's so much farther away. When the sun, the moon, and the Earth are aligned in a straight line, which happens during the full moon and new moon phases, the gravitational forces of the sun and the moon combine. This creates what we call spring tides. Spring tides have nothing to do with the season of spring—instead, the word "spring" comes from an old English word meaning "to jump or rise." During spring tides, the high tides are especially high, and the low tides are especially low because the gravitational forces are working together to pull the water more strongly.

On the other hand, when the sun and moon are at right angles to each other, which happens during the first and third quarters of the moon, their gravitational forces partially cancel each other out. This results in what we call neap tides. Neap tides are weaker than spring tides, with high tides that aren't as high and low tides that aren't as low. The difference between high and low tide during neap tides is much smaller, but the cycle continues just the same, with the ocean's waters rising and falling in a never-ending pattern.

The Atlantic Ocean, being one of the largest and most active bodies of water on Earth, experiences some of the most significant tides in the world. The size of the Atlantic, combined with its shape and the position of the continents that surround it, creates complex tidal patterns that can vary widely from one place to another. For example, in some parts of the Atlantic, like the Bay of Fundy in Canada, the tides are among the highest in the world. In the Bay of Fundy, the difference between high tide and low tide can be as much as 50 feet! This incredible tidal range is caused by the unique shape of the bay, which acts like a funnel, amplifying the effects of the tides as the water is forced into a narrower and narrower space.

In other parts of the Atlantic, the tides are much smaller, with only a few feet of difference between high and low tide. The Atlantic's tides are also affected by ocean currents, which can either enhance or reduce the strength of the tides depending on the direction they're flowing. For instance, the Gulf Stream, a powerful warm ocean current that flows from the Gulf of Mexico along the eastern coast of the United States and across the Atlantic toward Europe, can influence the tides by pushing water toward or away from the coastlines.

The tides in the Atlantic Ocean are also influenced by the rotation of the Earth. As the Earth spins on its axis, the positions of the high tides and low tides shift, creating a cycle that repeats approximately every 12 hours and 25 minutes. This means that in most places, there are two high tides and two low tides each day. However, in some parts of the world, including parts of the Atlantic, there is only one high tide and one low tide each day. This is called a diurnal tide, and it's less common than the more typical semidiurnal tide, which has two high and two low tides daily.

The impact of the Atlantic Ocean's tides on coastal areas is immense. For people living along the coast, the tides are a natural part of daily life. Fishermen, sailors, and beachgoers all pay close attention to the tides because they affect when and where they can safely go out on the water or access the beach. Harbors and ports are often designed to accommodate the changing tides, with boats and ships needing to time their arrivals and departures to coincide with high tide so they don't get stranded in shallow water. In some areas, special tide gauges are used to measure the height of the tides and predict when high and low tides will occur. This information is vital for navigation and for protecting coastal communities from flooding during unusually high tides.

Tides also play a crucial role in the ecosystems of the Atlantic Ocean. Many marine animals, including fish, crabs, and seabirds, rely on the changing tides to find food and shelter. In tidal zones, the areas of the shore that are exposed during low tide and covered during high tide, a rich variety of life thrives. When the tide goes out, it reveals a world of tide pools, where small fish, crabs, and sea anemones are trapped in pockets of water. These creatures must adapt to the changing environment, as they may be exposed to the air for several hours until the tide comes back in. For predators like seabirds and raccoons, low tide is the perfect time to hunt for food in these exposed areas.

Tidal marshes, which are coastal wetlands that are regularly flooded by the tides, are another important ecosystem found along the Atlantic Ocean. These marshes are teeming with life, providing a habitat for many species of fish, birds, and insects. The rising and falling tides help to circulate nutrients in the water, supporting the growth of plants and providing food for the animals that live there. Tidal marshes also play a crucial role in protecting coastal areas from erosion and flooding by acting as a buffer between the land and the ocean.

In addition to their ecological importance, the tides of the Atlantic Ocean are also a source of renewable energy. In some parts of the world, including parts of Europe and Canada, people have harnessed the power of the tides to generate electricity. Tidal power plants work by capturing the energy of the moving water as the tides rise and fall, using it to turn turbines and generate electricity. This clean, renewable energy source has the potential to provide a significant amount of power to coastal communities, reducing their reliance on fossil fuels and helping to combat climate change. However, tidal power is still a relatively new technology, and there are challenges to overcome, such as the potential impact on marine life and the cost of building tidal power plants.

While the tides of the Atlantic Ocean may seem predictable, they can also be influenced by other factors, such as weather patterns and storms. When strong winds or low-pressure systems move over the ocean, they can create storm surges, which are sudden and powerful rises in sea level that can cause flooding along the coast. Hurricanes, which are common in the Atlantic during the late summer and fall, can cause particularly destructive storm surges, with the force of the wind and the tides combining to create massive waves that can sweep over coastal areas and cause significant damage.

King tides are another example of how the tides can become more extreme under certain conditions. King tides occur when the gravitational pull of the moon and the sun is at its strongest, usually during a full moon or new moon when the moon is closest to Earth. These tides are much higher than normal, and in some areas, they can cause flooding even without a storm. King tides give us a glimpse of what sea levels might look like in the future as climate change causes the ocean to rise. Scientists study king tides to better understand how coastal areas might be affected by rising sea levels in the coming decades.

The study of tides, known as tidal science, is a complex and fascinating field. Scientists use a combination of satellites, tide gauges, and computer models to predict the tides and understand how they are changing over time. The tides are influenced by a wide range of factors, including the position of the moon and sun, the shape of the ocean floor, and the rotation of the Earth. By studying the tides, scientists can gain insights into everything from climate change to ocean circulation patterns.

In conclusion, the tides of the Atlantic Ocean are a powerful and essential part of our planet's natural systems. They are caused by the gravitational pull of the moon and sun, and they affect everything from the daily lives of coastal communities to the health of marine ecosystems. The Atlantic's tides are responsible for creating unique environments like tidal marshes and tide pools, and they even offer the potential for renewable energy through tidal power. While the tides may seem like a simple rise and fall of the ocean, they are actually the result of complex interactions between the Earth, the moon, and the sun. These mighty tides remind us of the incredible forces at work in our world and the many ways that the ocean shapes our lives. Whether you're walking along the beach at low tide or watching the waves crash against the shore during high tide, the tides are a constant reminder of the beauty and power of the Atlantic Ocean.

Chapter 6: Discovering the Gulf Stream

The Gulf Stream is one of the most important and powerful ocean currents on Earth, flowing like a giant, moving river within the Atlantic Ocean. It plays a vital role in shaping the climate, influencing weather patterns, and supporting marine life. The Gulf Stream has fascinated scientists and explorers for centuries due to its remarkable speed and the enormous impact it has, not just on the waters around it but on the lands it touches and even far beyond. Let's dive deep into the story of this mighty current, discovering what makes it so special and understanding how it works.

The Gulf Stream begins in the warm waters of the Gulf of Mexico, which is how it got its name. It flows from the Gulf, moving up the eastern coast of the United States before heading across the Atlantic Ocean toward Europe. The Gulf Stream is part of a larger system of ocean currents known as the North Atlantic Drift, and it stretches over 1,000 miles wide and is nearly 3,000 miles long, making it one of the most significant currents in the world. It is so powerful that the Gulf Stream moves about 100 times more water than all the rivers on Earth combined! That's a lot of water!

The Gulf Stream is driven by several different forces, including wind patterns, the rotation of the Earth, and differences in water temperature and salinity. It is a warm ocean current because it carries heat from the tropics, where the sun shines strongest, to the colder northern parts of the Atlantic. As the warm water moves, it not only affects the temperature of the ocean but also has a huge influence on the climate of the surrounding regions. For instance, the Gulf Stream keeps the east coast of North America warmer in the winter than it would otherwise be. Places like New York or even parts of Canada are milder in the winter months than other regions at the same latitude because of the heat carried northward by the Gulf Stream.

As the Gulf Stream moves across the Atlantic, it also affects Europe. Without the Gulf Stream, places like the United Kingdom and parts of northern Europe would be much colder, similar to the climate in Siberia! The warm waters of the Gulf Stream bring milder winters to Europe, allowing cities like London, Paris, and Berlin to have a more temperate climate even though they are located far from the equator. The Gulf Stream doesn't stop when it reaches Europe; it continues northward and helps to moderate the climate in places like Norway, where it brings warmth to the icy northern seas.

The Gulf Stream isn't just important for the climate. It also plays a key role in the global circulation of ocean water, a process often called the "global conveyor belt." This circulation helps distribute heat around the planet and regulates global climate patterns. The Gulf Stream is part of a larger system called the Atlantic Meridional Overturning Circulation (AMOC), which moves warm water from the tropics to the poles and cold water from the poles back to the equator. This massive, slow-moving circulation is essential for keeping the Earth's climate stable.

The Gulf Stream has an impressive speed. In some parts, it can move as fast as 5 miles per hour, which may not sound like much compared to how fast cars drive, but for an ocean current, that's extremely fast! The water in the Gulf Stream moves quickly because of the strong winds that blow from the west and push the surface waters. These winds are known as the trade winds and the westerlies. As the warm water flows northward, it also mixes with cooler water along its edges, creating swirling patterns of eddies and smaller currents that can stretch for miles.

The Gulf Stream has been known to people for centuries. Early sailors in the Atlantic discovered that the current could significantly speed up their journeys. In fact, European explorers like Christopher Columbus and later sailors in the age of discovery took advantage of the Gulf Stream's powerful current to travel more quickly across the ocean. Benjamin Franklin, one of the founding fathers of the United States, was among the first to map the Gulf Stream. He noticed that ships traveling to Europe from North America could save time if they stayed within the current, while those heading back to America would avoid it to make their journey easier. Franklin's early map of the Gulf Stream was one of the first scientific studies of ocean currents.

Marine life is also deeply affected by the Gulf Stream. The warm waters of the current create a rich environment for a variety of species, from tiny plankton to large fish and marine mammals. Because it carries warmer water into colder regions, the Gulf Stream acts like a conveyor belt for marine life, transporting nutrients and organisms across vast distances. Fish such as tuna, marlin, and swordfish thrive in the nutrient-rich waters of the Gulf Stream, making it an essential fishing ground for humans. Many species of migratory fish follow the Gulf Stream to find food and to spawn. Even larger creatures, like whales, follow the Gulf Stream's path as they migrate between feeding grounds.

But the Gulf Stream isn't just a highway for sea creatures—it also influences weather patterns. Storms that form in the Atlantic, such as hurricanes, can become more powerful as they move over the warm waters of the Gulf Stream. The heat from the current can fuel these storms, making them more intense and causing them to bring heavier rain and stronger winds to coastal areas. This is why hurricanes that travel over the Gulf Stream often grow in strength as they approach the eastern coast of the United States. Scientists monitor the Gulf Stream carefully, especially during hurricane season, to predict how it might influence storms and help people prepare for extreme weather.

The Gulf Stream is so powerful and important that changes to it can have far-reaching consequences. Scientists have been studying the Gulf Stream closely, especially in recent years, to understand how climate change might be affecting it. Some evidence suggests that the Gulf Stream may be slowing down due to the melting of ice in the Arctic. As more fresh water from melting ice flows into the Atlantic, it could disrupt the delicate balance of temperature and salinity that drives the Gulf Stream. If the Gulf Stream were to slow down significantly, it could lead to drastic changes in climate, not only for the Atlantic region but for the entire planet.

For example, if the Gulf Stream weakens, it could cause northern Europe to become much colder, with harsher winters and a drop in average temperatures. It could also disrupt weather patterns, leading to more extreme storms or changing rainfall patterns in parts of the world that depend on the Gulf Stream's influence. While it's unlikely that the Gulf Stream will stop altogether, even small changes to this powerful current could have a big impact on the global climate.

In addition to climate change, human activities like pollution and overfishing also affect the Gulf Stream. As more plastic and other pollutants enter the ocean, they can get caught up in the Gulf Stream and carried across vast distances. This pollution harms marine life and can disrupt ecosystems that depend on the Gulf Stream's flow. Overfishing in the waters around the Gulf Stream can also deplete fish populations, making it harder for both marine animals and humans to find food.

Despite these challenges, the Gulf Stream remains a crucial part of our planet's natural systems. Scientists continue to study it using satellites, ocean buoys, and other tools to learn more about how it works and how it might change in the future. Understanding the Gulf Stream is essential for predicting climate change, protecting marine life, and ensuring the safety of coastal communities that depend on the current's influence.

The Gulf Stream is a reminder of the incredible interconnectedness of our planet's oceans, atmosphere, and climate. It's a natural force that has shaped the world for millions of years and continues to play a vital role in our lives today. Whether we're standing on a beach feeling the warm waters brought by the Gulf Stream or watching a weather report about a storm influenced by the current, we are constantly reminded of the Gulf Stream's power and importance. As we learn more about this mighty current, we gain a deeper appreciation for the wonders of the ocean and the complex systems that keep our planet in balance.

So, the next time you think about the ocean, remember that there's a massive, warm river of water flowing through the Atlantic—the Gulf Stream—helping to shape our world in ways we might not even realize. Its warm currents, swift flow, and impact on weather and climate make it one of the most fascinating features of the Atlantic Ocean. It's a powerful reminder that the oceans are alive with movement and energy, constantly affecting the Earth in ways both big and small. Whether you're interested in marine biology, climate science, or just the wonders of nature, the Gulf Stream is an amazing and awe-inspiring part of our world.

Chapter 7: Sea Life of the Atlantic Ocean

The Atlantic Ocean is a vast and mysterious world teeming with an incredible diversity of sea life. From the sunlit surface waters to the dark, cold depths of the ocean floor, the Atlantic is home to a wide variety of creatures, many of which are still being discovered. The ocean is divided into different habitats, each offering unique conditions where specific animals, plants, and microorganisms can thrive. The sea life of the Atlantic plays a crucial role in the balance of marine ecosystems, contributing to the health of the planet and supporting the livelihoods of millions of people who rely on the ocean for food, transportation, and recreation.

One of the most well-known creatures in the Atlantic Ocean is the mighty blue whale, the largest animal on Earth. These gentle giants can grow up to 100 feet long and weigh as much as 200 tons. Despite their enormous size, blue whales feed on tiny shrimp-like animals called krill, consuming up to four tons of them each day. The blue whale's presence in the Atlantic reminds us of the incredible scale of life in the ocean, where the biggest animals depend on some of the smallest organisms for survival. The blue whale, along with other species of whales like humpbacks and fin whales, migrates through the Atlantic, traveling great distances between feeding and breeding grounds.

Dolphins, another beloved species, are often spotted in the Atlantic, especially near the coasts. These intelligent and playful animals live in social groups called pods and are known for their acrobatic leaps and friendly interactions with humans. Common species in the Atlantic include the bottlenose dolphin and the Atlantic spotted dolphin. Dolphins use echolocation to navigate and hunt for food, sending out sound waves that bounce back to them, allowing them to "see" their surroundings even in the dark or murky waters. Dolphins feed on fish and squid, often working together in their pods to catch prey. Their intelligence, social behavior, and playful nature make them one of the most fascinating creatures of the Atlantic Ocean.

The Atlantic is also home to many species of sharks, ranging from the fearsome great white shark to the gentle, plankton-feeding basking shark. Sharks are top predators in the ocean, playing a key role in maintaining the balance of marine ecosystems by controlling the populations of other species. The great white shark, which can grow up to 20 feet long, is known for its powerful jaws and sharp teeth, while the basking shark, the second-largest shark in the world, feeds by filtering tiny plankton from the water as it swims with its enormous mouth open. Other species of sharks found in the Atlantic include hammerheads, tiger sharks, and mako sharks, each adapted to life in different parts of the ocean.

In addition to large marine mammals and predators, the Atlantic is home to countless species of fish, ranging from tiny colorful reef fish to massive schools of tuna. One of the most famous fish in the Atlantic is the Atlantic cod, a species that has been a vital part of the fishing industry for centuries. Cod are bottom-dwelling fish that live in the colder waters of the North Atlantic and have been fished to near depletion in some areas due to overfishing. Efforts are now being made to protect cod populations through sustainable fishing practices, ensuring that this important species can continue to thrive in the Atlantic for generations to come.

Coral reefs, though more commonly associated with warmer oceans like the Pacific, are also found in the Atlantic, particularly in the Caribbean Sea. Coral reefs are some of the most biodiverse ecosystems on the planet, providing shelter and food for thousands of species of fish, invertebrates, and marine plants. Coral itself is made up of tiny animals called polyps, which build calcium carbonate skeletons that form the structure of the reef. Coral reefs in the Atlantic are home to brightly colored fish like parrotfish, angelfish, and butterflyfish, as well as invertebrates like sea anemones, sponges, and crabs. The reefs also support larger animals like sea turtles, which come to feed on the seagrasses and algae that grow around the coral.

Speaking of sea turtles, these ancient reptiles are another remarkable part of the Atlantic's sea life. The Atlantic is home to several species of sea turtles, including the leatherback, loggerhead, and green sea turtles. These turtles are known for their long migrations, with some species traveling thousands of miles between their nesting beaches and feeding grounds. Sea turtles face many threats, including habitat loss, pollution, and being caught accidentally in fishing nets. Conservation efforts are helping to protect these gentle creatures, ensuring that they continue to glide through the waters of the Atlantic for years to come.

The Atlantic Ocean is not only full of large, charismatic animals but also countless smaller creatures that are essential to the marine food web. Plankton, tiny organisms that drift with the ocean currents, are the base of the food chain. There are two main types of plankton: phytoplankton, which are microscopic plants that use sunlight to produce energy through photosynthesis, and zooplankton, tiny animals that feed on phytoplankton. These organisms are a vital food source for many larger marine animals, including fish, whales, and even some species of jellyfish.

Jellyfish are another common sight in the Atlantic Ocean, and while they may look delicate and otherworldly, they are well-adapted to life in the ocean. Jellyfish have been around for hundreds of millions of years, long before dinosaurs roamed the Earth. They move through the water by pulsating their bell-shaped bodies, and their tentacles are armed with stinging cells that they use to capture prey. Some jellyfish, like the Portuguese man o' war, have long, trailing tentacles that can deliver painful stings to humans, though most jellyfish are harmless. Jellyfish feed on small fish, plankton, and other marine organisms, and they are an important part of the food chain.

Another fascinating group of animals in the Atlantic are the cephalopods, which include octopuses, squids, and cuttlefish. These highly intelligent creatures are known for their incredible ability to change color and texture to blend into their surroundings, a skill that helps them avoid predators and sneak up on prey. The common octopus, found in the Atlantic, is a master of camouflage, able to change its appearance in the blink of an eye. Octopuses are also known for their problem-solving abilities, and they can use tools, open jars, and even escape from aquariums. Squids, on the other hand, are fast swimmers, propelling themselves through the water by expelling water from their bodies. The giant squid, which can grow up to 40 feet long, is one of the ocean's most mysterious creatures, rarely seen by humans.

The deeper regions of the Atlantic Ocean are home to some of the most bizarre and otherworldly creatures on the planet. In the abyssal depths, where sunlight never reaches and the pressure is immense, animals have evolved unique adaptations to survive in the extreme environment. One of the most famous deep-sea creatures is the anglerfish, which uses a bioluminescent lure to attract prey in the pitch-black darkness. These fish have large, sharp teeth and expandable stomachs that allow them to swallow prey much larger than themselves. Other deep-sea creatures include the vampire squid, which has glowing eyes and webbed arms, and the gulper eel, which has a gigantic mouth for catching food in the dark waters.

Hydrothermal vents, located along the ocean floor where tectonic plates meet, are another unique habitat in the Atlantic. These vents release superheated water rich in minerals, creating an environment where life thrives despite the lack of sunlight. Strange creatures like giant tube worms, which can grow up to 8 feet long, live around these vents, relying on bacteria that convert chemicals from the vents into energy in a process called chemosynthesis. These deep-sea ecosystems are some of the most extreme on Earth, yet they support a surprising diversity of life.

Seabirds are also a significant part of the Atlantic's ecosystem. Birds like puffins, albatrosses, and seagulls spend much of their lives at sea, hunting for fish and squid. Puffins, with their brightly colored beaks, are excellent divers, using their wings to "fly" underwater in search of food. Albatrosses, on the other hand, are known for their long wingspans and ability to glide for hours over the ocean without flapping their wings. These birds are important predators and scavengers, helping to keep the marine ecosystem in balance.

The Atlantic Ocean is not only home to a rich diversity of animals but also to an incredible variety of plants and algae. Seaweeds, like kelp, grow in the shallow waters along the coast, providing food and shelter for many marine animals. Seagrasses, which are flowering plants that grow in the ocean, form underwater meadows that are vital habitats for species like sea turtles, manatees, and fish. These underwater plants produce oxygen and help stabilize the ocean floor, preventing erosion and providing a nursery for young marine animals.

In addition to all the visible life in the Atlantic, there is a hidden world of microscopic organisms that play a crucial role in the health of the ocean. Bacteria and other microbes help break down organic matter, recycle nutrients, and support the food chain. Some of these microorganisms even produce oxygen through photosynthesis, contributing to the air we breathe. Without these tiny, unseen creatures, the Atlantic Ocean and the rest of the planet would be a very different place.

In conclusion, the sea life of the Atlantic Ocean is as vast and varied as the ocean itself. From the smallest plankton to the largest whales, the Atlantic is teeming with life in every corner, from the sunlit surface to the darkest depths. Each species plays a vital role in the complex web of marine ecosystems, contributing to the health and balance of the ocean. The diversity of sea life in the Atlantic is not only a testament to the resilience and adaptability of life on Earth but also a reminder of the importance of protecting our oceans for future generations.

Chapter 8: The History of Atlantic Shipwrecks

The history of Atlantic shipwrecks is a fascinating and often mysterious tale, filled with stories of adventure, tragedy, exploration, and even treasure. For centuries, the Atlantic Ocean has been one of the busiest and most important bodies of water in the world, serving as a highway for ships carrying goods, people, and ideas across continents. However, the vastness and unpredictability of the ocean have also made it a place of danger. Storms, navigation errors, warfare, and even piracy have caused thousands of ships to meet their fate on the bottom of the Atlantic. These shipwrecks are not just relics of the past but windows into history, offering clues about the lives of sailors, explorers, and passengers who traveled the seas in different eras.

One of the earliest known shipwrecks in the Atlantic dates back to ancient times. The Phoenicians, a seafaring people from what is now Lebanon, are believed to have explored the coasts of Europe and Africa long before many other civilizations. Archaeologists have discovered evidence of their ships being wrecked in the Atlantic as they traded goods like glass, purple dye, and metals. These early shipwrecks reveal the bravery and skill of ancient sailors who ventured into the unknown, often without the advanced navigation tools we have today. Their voyages set the stage for future exploration and trade across the Atlantic, but they also highlight the risks that came with sailing on the open ocean.

The Age of Exploration, which began in the 15th century, brought a new wave of shipwrecks as European explorers set out to discover new lands and trade routes. One of the most famous explorers, Christopher Columbus, crossed the Atlantic in 1492 and famously "discovered" the Americas, though indigenous peoples had been living there for thousands of years. During this time, many ships were lost to storms, reefs, and unknown dangers. One notable shipwreck was that of the Spanish ship *Santa Maria*, one of Columbus's vessels, which ran aground off the coast of present-day Haiti. The crew had to abandon the ship and build a fort, which was the first European settlement in the Americas. The loss of the *Santa Maria* marked one of the many shipwrecks that would follow as European powers explored and colonized the New World.

As trade between Europe, Africa, and the Americas flourished, more and more ships sailed across the Atlantic, and with them came the inevitable dangers of the sea. The Atlantic slave trade, a dark and tragic chapter in human history, also saw many shipwrecks. Ships carrying enslaved Africans to the Americas were often overcrowded and poorly built, leading to high death rates even before the ships reached their destinations. In some cases, these ships sank due to storms or other disasters. The wrecks of these ships are a grim reminder of the cruelty and inhumanity of the slave trade, and they hold the stories of countless individuals who never made it to shore.

Pirates also played a significant role in the history of Atlantic shipwrecks. During the so-called "Golden Age of Piracy" in the 17th and 18th centuries, pirates roamed the waters of the Caribbean and the Atlantic, attacking merchant ships and stealing valuable cargo. Many pirate ships themselves met their end in the treacherous waters of the Atlantic, either in battles with naval forces or by sinking due to poor maintenance. One of the most famous pirate shipwrecks is that of the *Queen Anne's Revenge*, the flagship of the infamous pirate Blackbeard. The *Queen Anne's Revenge* ran aground near the coast of North Carolina in 1718, and its remains were discovered in 1996. The shipwreck has since become an important archaeological site, offering a glimpse into the life of pirates and the dangers they faced.

During the 18th and 19th centuries, the Atlantic became an even busier maritime highway as ships carried goods like sugar, tobacco, and cotton from the Americas to Europe, and manufactured goods from Europe to the colonies. The Industrial Revolution also brought changes to shipbuilding, with iron and steel ships replacing wooden ones. Despite these advances, many ships continued to sink due to storms, collisions, and other accidents. One of the most famous shipwrecks from this period is the *SS Central America*, also known as the "Ship of Gold." This steamship sank off the coast of South Carolina in 1857 during a hurricane while carrying tons of gold from the California Gold Rush. The wreck of the *SS Central America* was discovered in 1988, and the gold recovered from the ship is estimated to be worth millions of dollars. This shipwreck is a reminder of both the fortunes won and lost at sea.

The Atlantic Ocean also became a theater of naval warfare during the 20th century, particularly during World War I and World War II. Both wars saw the sinking of numerous ships, from military vessels to civilian passenger ships. One of the most tragic shipwrecks of the early 20th century was the sinking of the RMS *Titanic* in 1912. The *Titanic*, considered an "unsinkable" ship, struck an iceberg on its maiden voyage and sank in the cold waters of the North Atlantic. More than 1,500 passengers and crew lost their lives in one of the deadliest maritime disasters in history. The story of the *Titanic* has captivated people for over a century, and its wreck, discovered in 1985, has been explored by scientists and historians eager to understand what went wrong.

World War II brought even more shipwrecks to the Atlantic, as German U-boats patrolled the ocean, sinking Allied ships in a campaign known as the Battle of the Atlantic. Many merchant ships, carrying vital supplies from North America to Europe, were targeted by the U-boats. One of the most famous shipwrecks from this period is the RMS *Lusitania*, a British ocean liner that was torpedoed by a German U-boat in 1915 during World War I. The sinking of the *Lusitania*, which resulted in the deaths of nearly 1,200 passengers, helped turn public opinion against Germany and contributed to the

United States entering the war. The wreck of the *Lusitania* lies off the coast of Ireland and is a haunting reminder of the horrors of war.

In addition to wartime shipwrecks, the Atlantic has also claimed many fishing and cargo ships over the years. The cold, rough waters of the North Atlantic are particularly dangerous for fishermen, who often face harsh weather conditions while working at sea. One of the most famous modern shipwrecks is that of the fishing vessel *Andrea Gail*, which was lost in the "Perfect Storm" of 1991 off the coast of Massachusetts. The story of the *Andrea Gail* was immortalized in the book and film *The Perfect Storm*, which tells the harrowing tale of the crew's final days as they battled towering waves and hurricane-force winds.

Treasure hunters and archaeologists continue to explore the wrecks of the Atlantic, searching for lost ships and the stories they hold. Some shipwrecks, like the *Atocha* and the *San José*, are believed to be laden with treasure, as they were Spanish galleons carrying gold and silver from the New World back to Spain. The *Atocha* was discovered in 1985 off the coast of Florida, and millions of dollars' worth of treasure was recovered. However, many shipwrecks remain undiscovered, hidden beneath the waves, waiting for the day when they might be found.

The history of Atlantic shipwrecks is not just a history of loss but also one of discovery. Each wreck tells a story of the people who sailed the ocean, the challenges they faced, and the world they lived in. From the ancient wrecks of the Phoenicians to the modern tragedies of fishing boats and ocean liners, shipwrecks are a testament to the power of the ocean and the bravery of those who have dared to cross it. Today, many of these wrecks are protected as historical sites, offering a glimpse into the past and reminding us of the incredible journeys that have taken place across the Atlantic Ocean.

Chapter 9: How Islands Form in the Atlantic

Islands in the Atlantic Ocean are incredible places, filled with beautiful landscapes, unique wildlife, and fascinating stories of how they came to be. But have you ever wondered how these islands formed in the first place? The process behind the formation of islands is complex and involves a variety of natural forces that shape our planet. From volcanic eruptions to shifting tectonic plates, islands can form in many different ways, and the Atlantic Ocean is home to some of the most interesting examples of island formation.

One of the most common ways that islands form in the Atlantic is through volcanic activity. Volcanoes are powerful forces of nature, and when they erupt, they can create new land. This process is known as volcanic island formation. Deep beneath the ocean's surface, magma (which is molten rock) rises up from the Earth's mantle through cracks in the ocean floor. When the magma reaches the surface, it cools and hardens, forming rock. Over time, layer after layer of hardened lava can build up until it rises above the surface of the water, creating a volcanic island.

One of the best-known examples of volcanic islands in the Atlantic is the Azores, a group of nine islands located about 850 miles west of Portugal. These islands were formed by volcanic activity over millions of years. Even today, the Azores have active volcanoes, and volcanic eruptions have shaped the islands' landscape, creating dramatic cliffs, craters, and lakes. In fact, some of the most beautiful parts of these islands, like the Lagoa do Fogo (Lake of Fire), are located in the calderas, or craters, of ancient volcanoes.

Another famous volcanic island group in the Atlantic is the Canary Islands, located off the northwest coast of Africa. The Canary Islands were also formed by volcanic activity, and some of their volcanoes are still active today. One of the most well-known volcanoes in the Canaries is Mount Teide, located on the island of Tenerife. Standing over 12,000 feet tall, Mount Teide is the highest peak in Spain and the third-highest volcano in the world when measured from its base on the ocean floor. The Canary Islands' volcanic origins have given them rugged landscapes and beautiful black sand beaches, which are made from volcanic rock.

Volcanic islands aren't the only type of islands that can form in the Atlantic, though. Some islands are formed by the movement of tectonic plates. Tectonic plates are massive pieces of the Earth's crust that float on the molten layer beneath the surface. These plates are constantly moving, although very slowly, and sometimes they collide or pull apart from one another. When tectonic plates move, they can create new landforms, including islands.

One way that tectonic plates can form islands is through a process called seafloor spreading. Seafloor spreading occurs when two tectonic plates move away from each other, creating a gap. Magma rises up from the Earth's mantle to fill the gap, and as it cools, it forms new crust. Over time, this new crust can build up and rise above the surface of the water, forming an island. This process is happening right now in the middle of the Atlantic Ocean at the Mid-Atlantic Ridge, a giant underwater mountain range that runs from the Arctic Ocean to the Southern Ocean.

The Mid-Atlantic Ridge is a fascinating place because it's where the Eurasian and North American tectonic plates, as well as the African and South American plates, are slowly moving apart from each other. In some places, the ridge rises above the surface of the ocean, creating islands. One of the most famous islands that formed this way is Iceland. Iceland is located right on top of the Mid-Atlantic Ridge, and its location makes it one of the most geologically active places on Earth. The island is still growing today as new land is formed by volcanic eruptions and seafloor spreading.

Another way that islands can form is through the action of coral reefs. Coral reefs are made up of tiny animals called coral polyps, which live in warm, shallow waters. These coral polyps build limestone skeletons around themselves, and over time, these skeletons pile up to form massive coral reefs. In some cases, coral reefs can grow large enough to become islands. This process is most common in tropical regions, but it can also happen in parts of the Atlantic.

Coral islands often form around the edges of underwater volcanoes. When a volcanic island forms, coral reefs can grow around its edges, creating a ring-shaped structure called an atoll. Over time, the volcano may sink back below the surface of the water, but the coral reef continues to grow, forming a low-lying coral island. The Bahamas, a group of over 700 islands in the Atlantic, are an example of islands that formed this way. The Bahamas are made mostly of coral and limestone, and their crystal-clear waters and sandy beaches are world-famous.

In addition to volcanic islands, tectonic islands, and coral islands, some islands in the Atlantic are formed by the accumulation of sand, mud, and other sediments. These are called barrier islands. Barrier islands are formed when ocean currents and waves move sand and sediment along the coast, creating long, narrow islands that run parallel to the mainland. These islands are often found along the eastern coast of the United States, where strong ocean currents have shaped the coastline over millions of years.

One famous example of a barrier island in the Atlantic is Cape Hatteras, located off the coast of North Carolina. Cape Hatteras is part of a chain of barrier islands known as the Outer Banks, which were formed by the action of wind and waves over thousands of years. Barrier islands like Cape Hatteras are constantly changing, as storms and ocean currents move sand from one place to another. Sometimes, barrier islands can even shift their position over time, moving closer to or farther away from the mainland.

The islands of the Atlantic are incredibly diverse, not just in how they were formed, but also in their landscapes and ecosystems. Some islands, like the volcanic islands of the Azores and the Canary Islands, have dramatic mountain ranges and lush forests. Others, like the coral islands of the Bahamas, are low-lying and surrounded by vibrant coral reefs teeming with marine life. And still others, like the barrier islands along the U.S. coast, are shaped by the constant movement of sand and sediment, creating ever-changing shorelines.

Islands also have rich cultural histories, shaped by the people who have lived on them for thousands of years. Many Atlantic islands have been home to indigenous peoples, explorers, settlers, and traders, each leaving their mark on the islands' history. For example, the Caribbean islands were home to indigenous peoples like the Taíno and Carib long before European explorers arrived in the 15th century. These islands became important centers of trade and colonization during the Age of Exploration, and their history is filled with stories of discovery, conflict, and cultural exchange.

Today, islands in the Atlantic continue to be important places for both people and wildlife. Some islands are home to unique species of plants and animals that can't be found anywhere else in the world. For example, the Galápagos Islands, located in the Pacific Ocean but influenced by Atlantic currents, are famous for their incredible biodiversity and the role they played in Charles Darwin's theory of evolution. Other islands, like the Falkland Islands and Greenland, are important for their natural resources and strategic locations.

Despite their beauty and importance, islands in the Atlantic are also vulnerable to the effects of climate change. Rising sea levels, stronger storms, and changing ocean temperatures all pose threats to island ecosystems and the people who live on them. For example, low-lying coral islands like those in the Bahamas are at risk of flooding and erosion as sea levels rise. Similarly, volcanic islands like those in the

Azores and the Canary Islands may experience more frequent volcanic activity and changing weather patterns due to climate change.

The formation of islands in the Atlantic is a reminder of the powerful forces that shape our planet, from volcanic eruptions to shifting tectonic plates to the slow accumulation of coral reefs. Each island has its own unique story, shaped by the natural processes that created it and the people and animals that call it home. As we continue to explore and study these islands, we learn more about the history of our planet and the incredible diversity of life that it supports.

Chapter 10: Atlantic Hurricanes and Storms

The Atlantic Ocean is a vast and mighty body of water, and with its great size and warm waters, it is the birthplace of some of the most powerful and fearsome storms on Earth: hurricanes. Hurricanes are huge, swirling storms with strong winds, heavy rains, and thunderous waves. These storms, known as tropical cyclones in scientific terms, can bring both awe and fear as they churn across the ocean, sometimes heading toward land where they can cause damage and devastation. But hurricanes aren't the only type of storms that form in the Atlantic. There are also tropical storms, which are similar to hurricanes but a little less powerful, and other weather systems like nor'easters and thunderstorms. Let's dive deep into the world of Atlantic hurricanes and storms to understand how they form, how they move, and the impact they can have.

To understand hurricanes, it helps to know a little bit about how the weather works. Hurricanes form when warm, moist air from the ocean rises up into the atmosphere. As the warm air rises, it leaves behind a low-pressure area near the surface of the ocean. Air from the surrounding areas rushes in to fill this low-pressure space, and as this air heats up, it also rises. This cycle repeats over and over, and as the warm, moist air continues to rise, it cools and condenses, forming clouds and releasing energy in the form of heat. This energy makes the storm grow stronger and stronger.

The process of hurricane formation typically starts with a tropical disturbance, which is a cluster of thunderstorms over warm ocean waters. If the conditions are just right, these thunderstorms can start to organize and spin, becoming what's called a tropical depression. At this stage, the system isn't very strong yet, but the winds start to pick up and the storm begins to rotate. If the tropical depression continues to strengthen, it can develop into a tropical storm. At this point, the winds are blowing at speeds of at least 39 miles per hour (63 kilometers per hour), and the storm gets a name from a pre-determined list of names that rotates each year. If the winds keep increasing and reach speeds of 74 miles per hour (119 kilometers per hour) or more, the tropical storm officially becomes a hurricane.

Hurricanes are categorized into different levels based on their wind speeds using something called the Saffir-Simpson Hurricane Wind Scale. This scale goes from Category 1, which is the least intense, to Category 5, which is the most powerful. A Category 1 hurricane has winds between 74 and 95 miles per hour (119 to 153 kilometers per hour), which can cause some damage to trees and buildings. A Category 5 hurricane, on the other hand, has winds of 157 miles per hour (252 kilometers per hour) or more, and it can cause catastrophic damage, with whole buildings being destroyed and trees uprooted. The stronger the hurricane, the more dangerous it is, not just because of the wind, but also because of the storm surge, which is a huge rise in sea level caused by the storm's winds pushing water toward the shore. Storm surges can cause massive flooding along coastlines and are often the deadliest part of a hurricane.

In the Atlantic Ocean, hurricane season runs from June 1 to November 30, though most hurricanes form between August and October when the ocean waters are at their warmest. Warm water is the fuel that powers hurricanes, so they need sea surface temperatures of at least 80 degrees Fahrenheit (27 degrees Celsius) to get going. That's why you won't see hurricanes forming in cold waters or in the winter. The Atlantic hurricane season is a time when weather forecasters are especially watchful because it's when tropical storms and hurricanes are most likely to develop and threaten coastal areas.

One of the most important parts of tracking and understanding hurricanes is knowing how they move. Hurricanes are steered by the winds around them, especially the trade winds and the jet stream. In the Atlantic, hurricanes typically form near the coast of Africa, where warm waters from the Atlantic Ocean meet the cool air from above. This area, known as the tropical Atlantic, is a common breeding ground for hurricanes. Once a storm forms, it is pushed westward by the trade winds, which blow from east to west in the tropics. As the hurricane moves across the Atlantic, it can grow stronger or weaker depending on the conditions it encounters. For example, if the hurricane moves over cooler water or hits land, it will start to weaken because it loses the warm water that fuels it. But if it stays over warm water and encounters little wind resistance, it can grow even stronger.

As hurricanes move westward, they often curve northward when they reach the Caribbean or the eastern coast of the United States. This curve is caused by the jet stream, a high-altitude wind current that moves from west to east across North America. The jet stream can either pull the hurricane northward and out to sea, or it can steer the storm toward land, where it can cause massive destruction. When hurricanes make landfall, they bring heavy rain, powerful winds, and storm surges that can flood coastal areas. Sometimes, even after the winds die down, the flooding caused by heavy rain can continue to cause problems for days.

The history of Atlantic hurricanes is filled with stories of massive storms that have shaped the lives of people living along the coasts. One of the most famous hurricanes in recent history was Hurricane Katrina, which struck the Gulf Coast of the United States in 2005. Katrina was a Category 5 storm at its peak and caused widespread destruction, particularly in the city of New Orleans, where levees (which are walls built to keep water out) failed, leading to catastrophic flooding. Thousands of people were displaced, and it took years for the region to recover. Another infamous storm was Hurricane Harvey in 2017, which brought record-breaking rainfall to Texas, causing massive flooding and billions of dollars in damage.

But not all hurricanes cause destruction. In fact, hurricanes play an important role in regulating the Earth's climate. They help to transport heat from the tropics to the poles, which helps to balance the planet's temperature. Without hurricanes, the tropics would get even hotter, and the poles would get colder. Hurricanes also help to bring much-needed rain to some areas, especially in places like the Caribbean, where the dry season can last for several months. In these regions, the rain brought by hurricanes and tropical storms can replenish water supplies and support agriculture.

Of course, hurricanes aren't the only storms that occur in the Atlantic. There are also tropical storms, which have wind speeds lower than hurricanes but can still cause heavy rain and flooding. Tropical storms are often a precursor to hurricanes, but not all of them grow strong enough to become hurricanes. Even though they are weaker than hurricanes, tropical storms can still cause a lot of damage, especially if they move slowly and dump large amounts of rain over one area.

In addition to hurricanes and tropical storms, the Atlantic is also home to another type of powerful storm called a nor'easter. Nor'easters are winter storms that affect the northeastern coast of the United States, usually between October and April. These storms get their name because the winds blow from the northeast, and they often bring heavy snow, rain, and strong winds to the region. While nor'easters aren't tropical storms, they can be just as dangerous, especially because they often occur in cold weather and can bring freezing temperatures and blizzard conditions.

Thunderstorms are also common in the Atlantic, especially during the summer months. Thunderstorms form when warm, moist air rises and cools rapidly, creating tall clouds and strong updrafts. These storms can produce lightning, heavy rain, and even tornadoes. While thunderstorms are usually smaller than hurricanes, they can still be dangerous, especially for sailors and people living near the coast.

Over the years, scientists and meteorologists have gotten better at predicting and tracking hurricanes and storms in the Atlantic. Today, satellites orbiting the Earth can track storms from space, providing real-time images of how they are developing and where they are headed. Advanced computer models can also predict the path of a storm, helping people in its potential path to prepare ahead of time. These predictions are crucial for saving lives and protecting property because they give people time to evacuate or take shelter before a storm hits.

In recent years, scientists have also been studying the impact of climate change on hurricanes. As the planet warms, sea surface temperatures are rising, which means that hurricanes could become more frequent and more intense. Warmer waters provide more energy for storms to grow, and rising sea levels can make storm surges even more dangerous. This means that the people living along the coasts of the Atlantic will need to be even more prepared for the possibility of stronger and more destructive hurricanes in the future.

The Atlantic Ocean's hurricanes and storms are a powerful reminder of the forces of nature. These storms, though fearsome, are a natural part of the Earth's weather system and play an important role in balancing the planet's climate. Through careful tracking and preparation, people living in hurricane-prone areas can stay safe and protect themselves from the dangers of these massive storms. From the early stages of a tropical disturbance to the full force of a Category 5 hurricane, the story of Atlantic hurricanes is one of nature's most dramatic and awe-inspiring phenomena.

Chapter 11: The Underwater Mountains and Ridges

The Atlantic Ocean is not just a vast expanse of water stretching from one continent to another—it is also home to incredible features hidden beneath the surface, like underwater mountains and ridges. These mountains and ridges are part of the Earth's seafloor and are just as fascinating and towering as the mountains we see on land. In fact, some underwater mountains are even taller than Mount Everest! Exploring the underwater terrain of the Atlantic reveals an amazing world that most people never see, where massive chains of mountains and ridges stretch for thousands of miles along the ocean floor. Let's dive deep into this underwater world to discover how these mountains and ridges form, what they look like, and why they are so important to life in the ocean.

One of the most remarkable features of the Atlantic Ocean is the Mid-Atlantic Ridge. This ridge is the longest mountain range on Earth, stretching from the Arctic Ocean in the north all the way down to the Southern Ocean near Antarctica. It runs almost like a spine right down the middle of the Atlantic Ocean and is thousands of miles long. But unlike the mountains we see on land, the Mid-Atlantic Ridge is mostly hidden beneath the waves, so you wouldn't know it was there just by looking at the ocean's surface. If you could somehow drain all the water from the Atlantic Ocean, you would see this giant underwater mountain range snaking its way through the middle of the ocean like a vast, winding backbone.

The Mid-Atlantic Ridge is what geologists call a "mid-ocean ridge." This means it's part of a system of underwater mountains that form where the Earth's tectonic plates—the huge slabs of rock that make up the Earth's crust—are slowly pulling apart. As these plates move away from each other, magma from deep inside the Earth rises up through the gap. When this hot, molten rock reaches the cold ocean water, it cools and hardens, forming new oceanic crust. Over time, as more magma rises and hardens, it builds up into a mountain range. This is how the Mid-Atlantic Ridge and other mid-ocean ridges are formed. It's like the Earth is constantly creating new land under the sea!

At the very top of the Mid-Atlantic Ridge, there is a long, deep valley called a "rift valley." This rift valley is the spot where the two tectonic plates are pulling apart. It's a deep, narrow trench that runs right down the center of the ridge, and it's one of the most geologically active places on Earth. As the plates continue to move, earthquakes often occur along the rift valley, shaking the seafloor. In some places, the Mid-Atlantic Ridge even rises above the ocean's surface to form islands. Iceland, for example, is one of the few places where you can actually see part of the Mid-Atlantic Ridge above water. The island sits right on top of the ridge, and it's still growing as new magma continues to push up from below.

The Mid-Atlantic Ridge is just one part of the underwater mountain ranges that crisscross the ocean floors. There are other underwater mountains, called seamounts, which are individual peaks that rise from the seafloor but don't break the surface of the water. These seamounts are often formed by volcanic activity, just like the Mid-Atlantic Ridge, but they are not connected to a ridge system. Seamounts can be towering structures, sometimes rising thousands of feet from the ocean floor. Some are dormant volcanoes, meaning they were once active but are no longer erupting. Others are still active, with occasional eruptions that release lava into the ocean.

While we can't see these underwater mountains with our eyes, scientists use special technology like sonar to map the seafloor and discover these hidden giants. Sonar works by sending sound waves down to the ocean floor and then measuring how long it takes for the sound to bounce back. The longer it takes, the deeper the ocean is at that point. By using sonar, scientists can create detailed maps of the underwater terrain, revealing mountains, valleys, ridges, and other features that would otherwise remain a mystery.

The mountains and ridges of the Atlantic Ocean are not just interesting geological features—they are also incredibly important for the creatures that live in the ocean. These underwater mountains create habitats for a wide variety of marine life. Many fish, corals, and other sea creatures live around seamounts and ridges because the mountains affect the ocean currents, bringing nutrient-rich water up from the deep sea to the surface. This process, called "upwelling," helps support thriving ecosystems around the mountains. Seamounts are often hotspots of biodiversity, meaning they are home to many different kinds of animals, some of which aren't found anywhere else in the ocean.

One of the most amazing creatures that live near underwater mountains is the deep-sea coral. Unlike the colorful corals that live in shallow, warm waters near tropical islands, deep-sea corals grow in cold, dark waters thousands of feet below the surface. These corals form intricate, tree-like structures that provide shelter and breeding grounds for fish and other marine animals. Some species of deep-sea corals are hundreds, or even thousands, of years old, making them some of the oldest living organisms on Earth. Because these corals grow so slowly, they are very vulnerable to damage from human activities like deep-sea fishing and mining, so it's important to protect them and the ecosystems they support.

In addition to supporting marine life, the mountains and ridges of the Atlantic also play an important role in the Earth's climate. The ocean currents that flow around the Mid-Atlantic Ridge help to regulate the Earth's temperature by distributing heat from the equator to the poles. These currents move warm water from the tropics toward the colder regions near the Arctic and Antarctic, and they bring cold water from the poles back down toward the equator. This circulation of water, known as the "global conveyor belt," helps to keep the Earth's climate stable. Without these underwater mountains and the currents they help guide, the Earth's climate would be much more extreme, with hotter temperatures near the equator and colder temperatures near the poles.

Another fascinating feature of the underwater mountains and ridges is that they are home to hydrothermal vents. Hydrothermal vents are cracks in the seafloor where superheated water, heated by magma below the Earth's crust, escapes into the ocean. These vents are like underwater geysers, releasing jets of boiling water and minerals into the surrounding water. Even though the water around these vents can be as hot as 750 degrees Fahrenheit (400 degrees Celsius), life thrives there. Strange creatures like giant tube worms, clams, and crabs live in the extreme environment around hydrothermal vents, surviving on the chemicals released by the vents instead of sunlight. This type of life, called "chemosynthesis," is one of the most unusual forms of life on Earth, and it shows just how adaptable living organisms can be.

The underwater mountains and ridges of the Atlantic also hold clues to the Earth's past. As scientists study the rocks and sediments that make up these features, they can learn about how the Earth's continents have shifted over millions of years. The theory of plate tectonics, which explains how the Earth's surface is divided into moving plates, was partly developed by studying the Mid-Atlantic Ridge and other underwater ridges. By examining the age of the rocks on either side of the ridge, scientists discovered that new oceanic crust is being created at the ridge and pushed outward, slowly moving the continents apart. This process, called "seafloor spreading," is still happening today and is one of the reasons why the Atlantic Ocean is slowly getting wider.

The formation of underwater mountains and ridges is an ongoing process that has been shaping the Earth for billions of years. As long as the tectonic plates continue to move and the Earth's mantle continues to produce magma, new mountains will continue to rise from the seafloor. In some places, these underwater mountains might eventually become islands, like the volcanic islands of the Azores or the Canary Islands, which were formed by volcanic activity along the Mid-Atlantic Ridge.

In summary, the underwater mountains and ridges of the Atlantic Ocean are some of the most incredible and mysterious features of our planet. From the immense Mid-Atlantic Ridge to the towering seamounts and hydrothermal vents, these underwater landscapes are home to diverse ecosystems, play a vital role in regulating the Earth's climate, and hold the secrets of the Earth's geological history. Even though we can't see these mountains with our own eyes, they are a crucial part of the Atlantic Ocean's story, and they remind us of the hidden wonders that lie beneath the surface of the sea.

Chapter 12: Exploring the Cold Waters of the North Atlantic

The North Atlantic Ocean is a vast and mysterious place, full of wonders both seen and unseen. Stretching from the icy Arctic Ocean down to the more temperate waters around Europe and North America, this part of the Atlantic is known for its cold waters, fierce weather, and breathtaking beauty. When you think of the North Atlantic, you might imagine vast, windswept seas, enormous waves crashing against rugged coastlines, and ships braving the icy waters. But there is so much more to explore in this chilly, awe-inspiring region.

The cold waters of the North Atlantic are primarily influenced by a combination of currents, wind patterns, and the geography of the surrounding landmasses. One of the most famous cold currents is the Labrador Current, which flows southward from the Arctic, carrying frigid water along the coast of Canada and the northeastern United States. This cold current is responsible for keeping the waters off places like Newfoundland and Nova Scotia chilly year-round. It also brings with it icebergs that have broken off from glaciers in Greenland and the Arctic. These floating giants can sometimes be seen drifting down the coast, silent reminders of the frozen north.

Icebergs are a unique and fascinating feature of the North Atlantic. These massive chunks of ice are formed when pieces of glaciers break off and float into the ocean. Most of an iceberg is hidden below the surface of the water—only about 10% is visible above. Some icebergs are small, no bigger than a car, while others can be as large as a skyscraper. These towering blocks of ice slowly melt as they drift southward, carried by the currents. Icebergs are not just beautiful to look at; they also pose serious dangers to ships. In 1912, the RMS Titanic, one of the most famous ships in history, struck an iceberg in the North Atlantic and sank, leading to one of the most tragic maritime disasters of all time.

The cold waters of the North Atlantic are also home to an incredible variety of marine life. Despite the frigid temperatures, the ocean here is teeming with life, from tiny plankton to massive whales. One reason the North Atlantic is so rich in marine life is because of the mixing of cold and warm waters. The cold Labrador Current meets the warmer Gulf Stream in the North Atlantic, creating nutrient-rich waters that support a thriving ecosystem. This mixing of currents helps bring nutrients up from the deep sea, providing food for tiny creatures like plankton, which in turn feed larger animals.

Some of the most iconic animals found in the cold waters of the North Atlantic are whales. This part of the ocean is a feeding ground for several species of whales, including the humpback whale, the minke whale, and the massive blue whale—the largest animal to have ever lived on Earth. Whales migrate to the North Atlantic during the summer months to feast on the abundant krill and small fish that swarm in these nutrient-rich waters. Humpback whales, with their acrobatic breaches and haunting songs, are especially famous for their impressive displays as they leap out of the water and splash back down with a tremendous crash. Watching a whale in the wild is an unforgettable experience, and the North Atlantic is one of the best places to see these magnificent creatures in their natural habitat.

But whales are not the only large creatures that call the cold waters of the North Atlantic home. Seals, porpoises, and dolphins are also common sights in these waters. Gray seals and harbor seals can often be seen lounging on rocky shores or swimming in the frigid waves. These marine mammals are well-adapted to the cold, with thick layers of blubber that help them stay warm in the icy water. Dolphins, like the playful Atlantic white-sided dolphin, are often spotted swimming alongside boats, leaping through the waves as if they are putting on a show for anyone lucky enough to be watching.

Fish are also abundant in the North Atlantic, and many of the species found here are important both to the ecosystem and to people. Cod, haddock, and herring are just a few examples of fish that thrive in these cold waters. In fact, the North Atlantic has been one of the most important fishing grounds in the world for centuries. Fishermen have been catching cod in the waters off Newfoundland and Iceland for hundreds of years, and these fish have played a key role in the economy and culture of the people who live along the coasts of the North Atlantic. However, overfishing has become a major problem in recent years, and efforts are being made to protect these valuable fish stocks and ensure that they can continue to thrive for future generations.

One of the most fascinating aspects of the North Atlantic is its connection to the weather. The cold waters of this region play a crucial role in shaping the climate not just in the North Atlantic itself, but across much of the Northern Hemisphere. The North Atlantic Oscillation, for example, is a climate pattern that affects weather conditions in Europe, North America, and even parts of Africa. Changes in the strength and position of the jet stream, which is influenced by the cold waters of the North Atlantic, can lead to cold, stormy winters in some years and milder, drier winters in others. The cold waters of the North Atlantic also help to drive the global ocean circulation system, sometimes called the "ocean conveyor belt," which moves warm and cold water around the planet and helps regulate the Earth's climate.

The North Atlantic is also known for its powerful storms. Some of the most intense and dangerous storms on Earth, known as Nor'easters, form in this region. These storms can bring heavy snow, rain, and strong winds to the northeastern United States and Canada. Nor'easters typically occur in the winter months when cold air from the Arctic meets warmer air from the Atlantic. The clash of these air masses creates a recipe for powerful storms that can dump feet of snow on coastal cities and cause dangerous conditions at sea.

Speaking of dangerous weather, the North Atlantic is also infamous for its role in the development of hurricanes. While hurricanes are more common in the warmer waters of the tropical Atlantic, some hurricanes do travel north and impact the colder regions of the North Atlantic. As these storms move north, they often weaken due to the cooler water temperatures, but they can still bring heavy rain, strong winds, and storm surges to coastal areas. In some cases, hurricanes can merge with other weather systems in the North Atlantic, transforming into even more powerful storms known as "extratropical cyclones."

But it's not just the cold waters and fierce weather that make the North Atlantic such an interesting place—it's also a region steeped in history and mystery. For centuries, explorers and sailors have braved the cold waters of the North Atlantic in search of new lands, trade routes, and adventure. Vikings were some of the first people to explore these waters, crossing the North Atlantic in their longships to reach places like Iceland, Greenland, and even North America, long before Christopher Columbus made his famous voyage. Later, European explorers like John Cabot and Henry Hudson ventured into the North Atlantic, searching for the fabled Northwest Passage—a route that would connect the Atlantic and Pacific Oceans through the Arctic.

The North Atlantic has also been the site of countless shipwrecks over the centuries. From the earliest Viking longships to modern-day vessels, many ships have met their end in these cold, unforgiving waters. Some shipwrecks, like the Titanic, are world-famous, while others remain lost to history, their stories waiting to be discovered by divers and explorers.

In addition to its natural beauty and historical significance, the North Atlantic is also home to many unique and beautiful islands. Iceland, one of the most well-known islands in the North Atlantic, is a land of fire and ice, with active volcanoes, massive glaciers, and stunning waterfalls. The Faroe Islands, located between Iceland and Norway, are another example of the rugged beauty of the North Atlantic. These islands are home to dramatic cliffs, windswept beaches, and a unique culture shaped by centuries of isolation.

The North Atlantic is a place of contrasts—where icy waters meet the warm currents of the Gulf Stream, where ancient shipwrecks lie beneath the waves, and where towering icebergs drift through the sea like frozen giants. It's a region of immense natural beauty and incredible diversity, home to some of the most fascinating marine life on the planet. From the cold, nutrient-rich waters that support thriving ecosystems to the powerful storms that shape the weather, the North Atlantic is a place of mystery, adventure, and wonder. Whether you're watching a pod of whales breach the surface or gazing at the majestic sight of an iceberg floating by, there's always something new and exciting to discover in the cold waters of the North Atlantic.

Chapter 13: The Role of the Atlantic in World Exploration

The Atlantic Ocean has played an enormous role in the history of world exploration. For thousands of years, it has been a pathway for explorers, adventurers, traders, and even conquerors who set sail in search of new lands, riches, and knowledge. The Atlantic has seen countless voyages that changed the course of history and helped shape the world as we know it today. From the earliest seafaring civilizations to the great age of exploration in the 15th and 16th centuries, the Atlantic has been central to humanity's understanding of geography, culture, and the possibilities of travel and trade.

One of the earliest groups to explore the Atlantic were the Phoenicians, a seafaring people from the ancient Mediterranean world. They were known for their incredible skill in navigation and shipbuilding, which allowed them to travel beyond the safety of coastal waters and into the more dangerous and unpredictable waters of the Atlantic. The Phoenicians were among the first to explore the western coasts of Africa, and their trade routes stretched as far as the British Isles. Although they didn't sail across the entire Atlantic Ocean, their ventures into the open sea helped set the stage for future exploration.

Another early seafaring group that explored the Atlantic were the Vikings. Around the 9th and 10th centuries, these Norse explorers, known for their longships and daring voyages, began sailing westward from Scandinavia. Led by famous figures like Leif Erikson, the Vikings explored the North Atlantic, discovering and settling places like Iceland and Greenland. In fact, they are believed to be the first Europeans to reach North America, landing in what is now Newfoundland, Canada, around the year 1000—centuries before Christopher Columbus. The Viking voyages across the North Atlantic were risky and dangerous, but they demonstrated that it was possible to travel across this vast ocean and reach new lands.

As time passed, the idea of exploration became even more enticing, especially during the 15th and 16th centuries. This period is known as the Age of Exploration, a time when European nations, particularly Spain and Portugal, were driven by a desire to discover new trade routes, spread Christianity, and find untold wealth in the form of gold, spices, and other valuable goods. The Atlantic Ocean became the focal point of this age, as it was the body of water that separated Europe from the mysterious and unknown lands to the west.

One of the most famous explorers of the Atlantic during this time was Christopher Columbus. In 1492, Columbus set sail from Spain, determined to find a westward route to Asia, but instead, he stumbled upon the islands of the Caribbean, marking the beginning of European exploration and colonization of the Americas. Columbus's voyage across the Atlantic was a turning point in world history. It connected Europe with the Americas for the first time and opened up new opportunities for trade, conquest, and cultural exchange. After Columbus, other explorers followed in his wake, eager to claim new territories and establish trade routes across the Atlantic.

The exploration of the Atlantic didn't stop with Columbus. Portuguese explorers, like Vasco da Gama, sought to find a sea route to India by sailing around the southern tip of Africa. Although this route went through the Indian Ocean, the journey started in the Atlantic, and it was another example of how the Atlantic Ocean was the starting point for some of the most important exploration voyages of the time. Portuguese navigators also played a key role in mapping the coasts of Africa and Brazil, establishing important trade routes across the Atlantic that linked Europe, Africa, and the Americas.

One of the most dramatic effects of Atlantic exploration was the so-called Columbian Exchange, which refers to the massive exchange of goods, people, animals, plants, and even diseases between the Old

World (Europe, Africa, and Asia) and the New World (the Americas) following Columbus's voyages. This exchange had a profound impact on the cultures and economies of both sides of the Atlantic. European settlers brought crops like wheat, rice, and sugarcane to the Americas, while American crops like potatoes, maize (corn), and tomatoes were introduced to Europe. Animals like horses, cattle, and pigs were also brought to the New World, where they transformed the way indigenous people lived and worked. Unfortunately, this exchange also included the spread of diseases like smallpox, which had devastating effects on the native populations of the Americas.

In addition to the exchange of goods, the Atlantic also became a highway for human migration—both voluntary and forced. The Atlantic slave trade, which took place from the 16th to the 19th centuries, was one of the darkest chapters in the history of the Atlantic Ocean. European traders forcibly transported millions of Africans across the Atlantic to the Americas, where they were sold into slavery to work on plantations and in mines. The Middle Passage, as this journey was called, was a horrific experience for the enslaved Africans, many of whom did not survive the journey. The slave trade had a lasting impact on the cultures and economies of the Americas, Africa, and Europe, and it remains a painful legacy of Atlantic exploration and exploitation.

Despite the horrors of the slave trade, the Atlantic also facilitated more positive exchanges of culture and ideas. As European explorers continued to map the Atlantic, they established colonies and trade networks that spanned the globe. The Atlantic became a critical part of the global economy, as goods like sugar, tobacco, and cotton were shipped from the Americas to Europe, while European manufactured goods were sent back across the ocean. This trade network brought immense wealth to European nations and helped fuel the growth of powerful empires.

The Atlantic's role in world exploration wasn't just limited to European nations. In the late 18th and early 19th centuries, the newly independent United States of America began to explore the Atlantic and establish its own presence on the world stage. American sailors ventured across the ocean to trade with European nations, while explorers like Lewis and Clark traveled westward across the continent in search of new opportunities. The Atlantic was also a key theater during the War of 1812, when American and British ships fought for control of the seas.

Throughout the 19th and 20th centuries, the Atlantic continued to be a major route for exploration and discovery. Advances in navigation, shipbuilding, and technology made transatlantic travel faster and safer. Explorers like Charles Lindbergh crossed the Atlantic by air, becoming the first person to fly nonstop from New York to Paris in 1927. This feat marked a new era in transatlantic travel, as airplanes began to replace ships as the primary means of crossing the ocean.

The Atlantic Ocean has not only been a pathway for human exploration but also a source of scientific discovery. Oceanographers and marine biologists have studied the Atlantic's depths, discovering new species of fish and other marine life. The ocean floor has been mapped using sonar and other advanced technologies, revealing the existence of underwater mountain ranges, deep trenches, and vast plains. One of the most significant scientific discoveries in the Atlantic was the Mid-Atlantic Ridge, a massive underwater mountain range that runs down the center of the ocean. This ridge is part of the system of tectonic plates that make up the Earth's crust, and it is where new oceanic crust is formed as molten rock rises from the Earth's mantle.

The Atlantic has also played a crucial role in the development of communication technology. In the 19th century, the first transatlantic telegraph cables were laid across the ocean floor, allowing for nearly instant communication between Europe and North America. This technological achievement revolutionized the way people communicated and helped shrink the world, making it easier for nations on opposite sides of the Atlantic to share information and ideas.

In the modern world, the Atlantic Ocean continues to be a vital route for travel, trade, and exploration. Ships still cross the Atlantic every day, carrying goods between continents, while airplanes fly thousands of passengers across the ocean to destinations all over the world. Scientists continue to study the Atlantic's currents, marine life, and geological features, seeking to learn more about this vast and complex body of water. The Atlantic's role in exploration may have changed over the centuries, but it remains just as important today as it was during the age of Columbus and the Vikings.

The history of the Atlantic Ocean is one of adventure, discovery, and cultural exchange. From the earliest seafaring civilizations to the technological advances of the modern era, the Atlantic has been a bridge between continents, connecting people, ideas, and goods. It has shaped the course of world history in ways that are still being felt today, and its role in exploration and discovery will continue to inspire generations of explorers, scientists, and adventurers for years to come.

Chapter 14: The Atlantic Ocean's Coral Reefs

The Atlantic Ocean's coral reefs are some of the most fascinating and important ecosystems on Earth. They may not be as large or famous as the coral reefs found in the Pacific or Indian Oceans, like the Great Barrier Reef in Australia, but they are still home to a rich diversity of marine life and play a crucial role in maintaining the health of the ocean. Coral reefs are often called the "rainforests of the sea" because of their incredible biodiversity. These underwater habitats are made up of millions of tiny coral polyps, which are small, soft-bodied animals related to jellyfish. When coral polyps gather in large numbers and secrete calcium carbonate, they form the hard, stony structures we recognize as coral reefs.

The Atlantic Ocean is home to several notable coral reef systems, including those in the Caribbean Sea and the waters surrounding Florida, the Bahamas, Bermuda, and parts of the South American coastline. The warm, shallow waters of these regions provide the perfect conditions for coral reefs to thrive. Coral reefs need sunlight to grow, which is why they are typically found in shallow waters, usually no deeper than 150 feet (45 meters). These sunlit waters allow the tiny algae, called zooxanthellae, that live within the coral polyps to carry out photosynthesis. This process provides energy and nutrients to the coral, enabling it to grow and build the complex structures that form the foundation of the reef ecosystem.

One of the most well-known coral reefs in the Atlantic is the Florida Reef, the only living coral barrier reef in the continental United States. It stretches about 360 miles (580 kilometers) along the southeastern coast of Florida, from the Dry Tortugas near Key West to the St. Lucie Inlet. This reef system is part of the larger Mesoamerican Barrier Reef System, which extends into the Caribbean Sea and is the second-largest coral reef system in the world, after the Great Barrier Reef. The Florida Reef is a vital habitat for countless species of fish, invertebrates, and other marine organisms. It also serves as a natural barrier, protecting Florida's coastline from storm surges and waves generated by hurricanes and other storms.

The Caribbean Sea, which is part of the Atlantic Ocean, is home to some of the most vibrant and diverse coral reefs in the world. Countries like Belize, the Dominican Republic, Cuba, and Jamaica are famous for their stunning coral reefs, which attract divers and snorkelers from all over the globe. The Belize Barrier Reef, a UNESCO World Heritage Site, is particularly famous. Stretching over 190 miles (300 kilometers) along the coast of Belize, this reef is a critical habitat for a wide variety of marine life, including endangered species like sea turtles, manatees, and the Nassau grouper. The reef is also known for its beautiful coral formations and crystal-clear waters, making it one of the top destinations for underwater exploration.

The coral reefs of the Atlantic are not only beautiful; they are also incredibly important to the health of the ocean. Coral reefs provide a home and breeding ground for many species of fish, invertebrates, and other marine organisms. Some of these species are commercially important, meaning that they are caught by fishermen and sold as food. Without coral reefs, many of these species would struggle to survive, which would have a huge impact on the fishing industry and the people who depend on it for their livelihoods. Coral reefs also help to regulate the levels of carbon dioxide in the ocean by storing carbon in the form of calcium carbonate. This process helps to mitigate the effects of climate change by reducing the amount of carbon dioxide in the atmosphere.

However, coral reefs in the Atlantic Ocean, like those around the world, are facing serious threats. One of the biggest threats to coral reefs is climate change. As the Earth's temperature rises due to the buildup of greenhouse gases in the atmosphere, the temperature of the ocean also rises. Corals are very sensitive to changes in temperature, and even a small increase in water temperature can cause them to become stressed. When coral is stressed, it expels the zooxanthellae that live within its tissues, which causes the coral to turn white, a phenomenon known as coral bleaching. Without the algae to provide nutrients, the coral can die if the water remains too warm for too long.

Coral bleaching events have become more frequent and severe in recent years, especially in the Atlantic and Caribbean regions. In 2005, for example, a massive coral bleaching event occurred in the Caribbean, affecting over 80 percent of coral reefs in the region. Many of these corals never fully recovered. Climate change is also causing the oceans to become more acidic due to the increased levels of carbon dioxide in the atmosphere. Ocean acidification makes it harder for corals to produce their calcium carbonate skeletons, which weakens the reefs and makes them more vulnerable to damage from storms, disease, and human activities.

Another major threat to coral reefs in the Atlantic is pollution. Runoff from agriculture, sewage, and industrial activities can introduce harmful chemicals and nutrients into the ocean, which can damage coral reefs. Nutrient pollution, in particular, can lead to the growth of algae that smother corals and block out sunlight, preventing them from carrying out photosynthesis. In addition to pollution, overfishing can also harm coral reefs. Many fish species that live on coral reefs play important roles in maintaining the balance of the ecosystem. For example, parrotfish help to keep algae in check by feeding on it, which allows the corals to thrive. If these fish are overfished, algae can grow out of control and harm the reef.

Coral reefs in the Atlantic are also threatened by physical damage from human activities. Tourism, for example, is a major industry in many parts of the Caribbean, and while it brings economic benefits, it can also have negative effects on coral reefs. Divers, snorkelers, and boaters can accidentally damage coral by touching or stepping on it, and the anchors from boats can break off pieces of coral. In some areas, coral is even harvested for use in jewelry or souvenirs, further depleting the reefs.

Despite these threats, efforts are being made to protect and restore coral reefs in the Atlantic. Marine protected areas (MPAs) have been established in many parts of the region, including the Florida Keys National Marine Sanctuary, which helps to safeguard the coral reefs in the Florida Reef system. In these protected areas, fishing and other harmful activities are restricted, allowing the reefs to recover and thrive. Scientists are also working on coral restoration projects, which involve growing corals in nurseries and transplanting them onto damaged reefs. These efforts have shown promise in helping to rebuild coral populations and restore the health of the reefs.

Another important conservation strategy is educating the public about the importance of coral reefs and the steps they can take to protect them. Simple actions like reducing water pollution, practicing sustainable fishing, and being mindful of marine life when diving or snorkeling can make a big difference in preserving these fragile ecosystems. Additionally, addressing the root causes of climate change by reducing carbon emissions and switching to renewable energy sources is critical for ensuring the long-term survival of coral reefs in the Atlantic and around the world.

In conclusion, the coral reefs of the Atlantic Ocean are vital ecosystems that support a rich diversity of marine life and provide numerous benefits to people and the planet. From the vibrant reefs of the Caribbean to the important barrier reefs of Florida, these underwater habitats are both beautiful and essential. However, they are also facing serious threats from climate change, pollution, overfishing, and physical damage. Protecting and preserving the coral reefs of the Atlantic requires a concerted effort from individuals, governments, and organizations around the world. By working together, we can ensure that these amazing ecosystems continue to thrive for generations to come.

Chapter 15: Protecting the Atlantic from Pollution

Protecting the Atlantic Ocean from pollution is a critical and urgent task. The Atlantic is one of the largest and most vital bodies of water on Earth, covering about 20% of the planet's surface. Its waters are home to countless marine species, and its currents play a major role in regulating the Earth's climate. The ocean is also essential for human life, providing food, oxygen, and a means of transportation. However, over the years, pollution has become one of the greatest threats to the health of the Atlantic. From plastic waste and chemical runoff to oil spills and noise pollution, the Atlantic faces many challenges, and it's up to all of us to protect this incredible resource for future generations.

One of the most significant types of pollution affecting the Atlantic Ocean is plastic waste. Every year, millions of tons of plastic enter the ocean, and the Atlantic is no exception. Plastic pollution comes from many sources, including discarded bottles, bags, fishing nets, and microplastics—tiny particles that come from things like cosmetic products and the breakdown of larger plastic items. Unlike organic materials, plastic doesn't biodegrade; instead, it breaks down into smaller and smaller pieces, which can persist in the ocean for hundreds of years. These plastic particles can be mistaken for food by marine animals, leading to ingestion, which can cause injury or even death. Birds, fish, sea turtles, and marine mammals are all affected by plastic pollution, with some becoming entangled in fishing nets or other debris.

One of the most visible signs of plastic pollution in the Atlantic is the North Atlantic Garbage Patch, a large area in the ocean where plastic waste accumulates due to the ocean's currents. While it isn't a solid mass of trash, like some people imagine, it's still a massive collection of floating debris, primarily plastic, that poses a serious threat to marine life. Fish, seabirds, and other animals can become trapped in or ingest the debris, which can lead to suffocation, starvation, or poisoning. The plastic can also absorb harmful chemicals, which then enter the food chain, eventually making their way to humans who consume seafood.

Chemical pollution is another major problem in the Atlantic Ocean. Runoff from agriculture, industry, and urban areas carries harmful chemicals like pesticides, fertilizers, heavy metals, and toxic industrial waste into rivers and streams, which eventually flow into the ocean. These chemicals can have devastating effects on marine ecosystems. For example, excess nutrients from fertilizers can lead to a phenomenon called eutrophication, where algae grow rapidly on the surface of the water, blocking sunlight from reaching the organisms below. When the algae die and decompose, they consume large amounts of oxygen, creating "dead zones" where marine life cannot survive.

One of the most infamous dead zones is found in the Gulf of Mexico, which is part of the Atlantic Ocean. Every summer, a massive dead zone forms due to nutrient pollution carried by the Mississippi River. This dead zone can cover thousands of square miles and has severe consequences for the fish and other creatures that rely on the ocean for their survival. The fish either have to flee the area, or they suffocate and die due to the lack of oxygen. This not only affects marine ecosystems but also impacts local fishing industries, which depend on healthy fish populations.

Oil spills are another major source of pollution in the Atlantic. When oil spills occur, either from drilling operations, pipeline ruptures, or tanker accidents, they release huge amounts of crude oil into the ocean. This oil spreads across the surface of the water, creating thick, sticky layers that suffocate marine life and contaminate coastal habitats. One of the most famous oil spills in the Atlantic was the Deepwater Horizon disaster in 2010, which occurred in the Gulf of

Mexico. The spill released millions of barrels of oil into the ocean over the course of several months, causing widespread damage to marine ecosystems and wildlife. Birds, sea turtles, dolphins, and fish were all affected by the spill, and some populations have still not fully recovered.

Oil spills can also have long-term effects on the ocean's ecosystem. Oil that sinks to the bottom of the ocean can smother coral reefs and other benthic (seafloor) habitats, while the toxins in the oil can accumulate in the bodies of fish and other marine animals. These toxins can then move up the food chain, potentially affecting humans who consume seafood contaminated by the spill. Cleaning up oil spills is a complex and difficult process, often requiring a combination of chemical dispersants, skimming devices, and even manual labor to remove the oil from the water and affected coastlines.

Noise pollution is another less visible but increasingly important issue in the Atlantic Ocean. The constant hum of ships, submarines, and oil drilling operations can disrupt marine animals' ability to communicate, navigate, and find food. Whales, dolphins, and other marine mammals rely on sound to communicate and orient themselves in the vast, dark ocean. The noise from human activities can drown out their calls, leading to disorientation, stress, and even strandings. In some cases, loud underwater explosions from oil exploration and military exercises can cause direct harm to marine animals, damaging their hearing or causing internal injuries.

To protect the Atlantic Ocean from pollution, we need to take a variety of actions, both individually and collectively. One of the most important steps is reducing our use of plastic. By choosing reusable items like water bottles, shopping bags, and containers, we can cut down on the amount of plastic waste that ends up in the ocean. Recycling is also critical—by ensuring that plastic is properly recycled, we can prevent it from entering landfills and eventually making its way into the ocean. Additionally, supporting legislation that bans single-use plastics, such as plastic straws and cutlery, can make a significant difference in reducing plastic pollution.

On a larger scale, industries need to adopt cleaner, more sustainable practices. Agriculture and industry are major contributors to chemical pollution, so finding ways to reduce runoff is key. For example, farmers can use precision agriculture techniques to apply fertilizers and pesticides more efficiently, minimizing the amount of excess chemicals that end up in rivers and oceans. Industries should also be held accountable for properly treating and disposing of hazardous waste, rather than dumping it into waterways.

In terms of oil pollution, reducing our reliance on fossil fuels can help prevent spills and other forms of pollution associated with oil extraction and transportation. Transitioning to renewable energy sources like wind, solar, and hydroelectric power not only helps reduce carbon emissions but also minimizes the need for risky offshore drilling operations. Governments can also enforce stricter safety regulations for oil drilling and shipping, ensuring that companies take the necessary precautions to prevent spills and respond quickly when accidents do occur.

Protecting marine life from noise pollution is another critical step in safeguarding the Atlantic. Regulations can be put in place to limit the noise levels produced by ships, oil rigs, and other human activities in sensitive marine habitats. For example, shipping companies can be required to adopt quieter engine technologies and modify their shipping routes to avoid areas where marine animals are known to gather, such as whale breeding grounds. Additionally, limiting the use of sonar and underwater explosives for military and industrial purposes can help reduce the impact of noise pollution on marine mammals.

Marine protected areas (MPAs) are another essential tool for preserving the health of the Atlantic. These designated zones limit human activities such as fishing, drilling, and shipping, allowing ecosystems to recover and thrive. There are already several MPAs in the

Atlantic, but expanding these areas and enforcing protections is crucial for ensuring the long-term health of the ocean. MPAs not only protect marine life from pollution but also help preserve biodiversity, protect endangered species, and allow overfished populations to recover.

Education and awareness are also key in the fight to protect the Atlantic Ocean from pollution. Teaching people about the importance of the ocean and the impact of pollution can inspire individuals to take action and make more sustainable choices in their daily lives. Schools, organizations, and governments can all play a role in raising awareness about ocean pollution and encouraging environmentally friendly behaviors. For example, beach cleanups are a great way for communities to come together and remove trash from the coastline before it has a chance to enter the ocean.

In conclusion, the Atlantic Ocean is facing a wide range of pollution-related challenges, from plastic waste and chemical runoff to oil spills and noise pollution. These issues threaten the health of marine ecosystems and the animals that depend on them, as well as the people who rely on the ocean for food, livelihoods, and recreation. However, by taking action at both the individual and collective levels, we can work to protect this vital resource. Reducing plastic waste, minimizing chemical runoff, transitioning to cleaner energy sources, and protecting marine habitats are all important steps in safeguarding the Atlantic Ocean for future generations. It's up to all of us to act now and make a difference before it's too late.

Chapter 16: Amazing Facts About Atlantic Waves

The Atlantic Ocean is full of amazing wonders, and one of the most incredible features of this vast body of water is its waves. Waves are not only fascinating to watch as they roll and crash against the shore, but they are also incredibly powerful and can travel thousands of miles across the ocean. The waves in the Atlantic are driven by winds, the rotation of the Earth, and even the gravitational pull of the moon and sun. Understanding the amazing facts about Atlantic waves reveals how much they shape the ocean, its ecosystems, and the lives of people living along its shores.

To begin with, waves in the Atlantic Ocean can vary greatly in size. Some are small and gentle, barely noticeable as they ripple across the water's surface. Others are enormous, towering over ships and even buildings, creating awe-inspiring sights. The size of a wave depends on several factors, including how strong the wind is, how long the wind has been blowing, and how far the wave has traveled. Waves that form far out in the open ocean can grow to tremendous heights, especially if they are caught up in storms or strong winds. These waves, called "swell," can travel for thousands of miles before finally reaching land.

One of the most important things to understand about waves is that they are not made of water traveling across the ocean. Instead, the energy moves through the water, causing it to rise and fall in a circular motion. Imagine it like a group of people doing the wave at a sports game—the people themselves don't move from their seats, but the motion of the wave travels around the stadium. In the same way, water particles don't travel across the ocean when a wave forms; they simply move up and down as the wave passes through them. This energy can come from wind, earthquakes, or even volcanic eruptions under the sea.

In the Atlantic Ocean, some of the most powerful and awe-inspiring waves are created by storms, particularly hurricanes. Hurricanes are massive storms that form over warm ocean waters, and they can generate waves as high as 60 feet (about 18 meters) or more. These massive waves can cause serious damage to ships and coastal areas, and they are a reminder of the immense power of the ocean. Even though hurricanes are dangerous, they also show how wind, water, and energy interact to create some of the most spectacular natural phenomena on Earth.

Another amazing fact about waves in the Atlantic is how far they can travel. Waves that are formed by winds in the southern part of the Atlantic can travel all the way to the northern coasts of Europe and North America. This is because waves can keep going long after the wind that created them has died down. These long-traveling waves are called "swell," and they can be smooth and regular, unlike the choppy waves you see near a storm. Surfers love to ride swells because they create perfect, long-lasting waves that are ideal for catching and riding to shore.

The Atlantic Ocean is also home to a famous region known for its big and dangerous waves—the North Atlantic, particularly around the area of Cape Horn. This part of the ocean is notorious for its rough seas and enormous waves, some of which can reach up to 100 feet (about 30 meters) high during the worst storms. Sailors have feared this part of the Atlantic for centuries, and even with modern ships and technology, it remains a challenging and dangerous area to navigate. The cold waters, powerful winds, and swirling currents combine to create some of the largest and most dangerous waves in the world.

One of the most fascinating types of waves in the Atlantic Ocean is known as "rogue waves." Rogue waves are massive, unpredictable waves that can appear out of nowhere, towering over the surrounding ocean. These waves can be twice as large as the other waves around them and can pose a serious danger to ships and boats. Scientists are still trying to understand exactly how rogue waves form, but many believe that they occur when waves combine in just the right way to create a super-sized wave. Rogue waves have been known to reach heights of over 100 feet (30 meters), and they are responsible for the mysterious disappearance of many ships throughout history.

Another incredible fact about Atlantic waves is how they affect the coastline. Over time, waves can shape the land, eroding cliffs, beaches, and rocks, and creating new formations. The constant pounding of waves on the shore causes erosion, breaking down rocks and sand and carrying them away. In some places, waves can even create new landforms, like sandbars, dunes, and beaches. These processes happen slowly, over hundreds or even thousands of years, but they show just how powerful waves can be in shaping the environment.

Waves also play a vital role in marine ecosystems. As waves move through the water, they mix the surface water with deeper layers of the ocean, helping to circulate nutrients and oxygen. This is especially important for marine life, such as plankton, fish, and other creatures that depend on these nutrients to survive. The movement of waves helps bring oxygen-rich water to deeper areas of the ocean, which is essential for the health of marine animals. Waves also help disperse plankton, which forms the base of the food chain in the ocean, and they provide food and habitat for fish and other animals that live near the surface.

In addition to their role in marine ecosystems, waves are also important for humans. For centuries, people have used the power of waves to travel across the ocean. Early explorers and traders relied on wind and waves to guide their ships as they crossed the Atlantic, and even today, waves are a critical part of maritime travel. Fishermen also depend on waves to bring fish closer to the surface, where they can be caught more easily. In some parts of the world, waves are even used to generate electricity through wave energy, which harnesses the power of the ocean to create renewable energy.

One of the most interesting aspects of waves is their connection to the moon. The gravitational pull of the moon is responsible for creating tides, which are the regular rise and fall of the ocean's surface. While tides are not technically waves, they are closely related, as the movement of tides can create waves along the shore. The moon's gravitational force causes the water in the Atlantic to bulge toward it, creating a high tide. As the Earth rotates, the high tide moves around the planet, creating waves and currents that shape the ocean's surface.

Waves also have a cultural significance. Throughout history, humans have been fascinated by the power and beauty of waves, and they have often been featured in art, literature, and folklore. From the ancient Greeks, who believed that the god Poseidon controlled the seas and waves, to modern-day surfers who chase the perfect wave, waves have captured the imagination of people all over the world. In some cultures, waves are seen as symbols of strength, change, or even danger, while in others, they are celebrated for their beauty and rhythm.

Surfers, of course, are among the people most fascinated by waves. The Atlantic Ocean is home to some of the best surfing spots in the world, including places like the East Coast of the United States, Portugal, and the Canary Islands. Surfers travel from all over the world to catch the perfect Atlantic wave, riding swells that have traveled thousands of miles to reach the shore. For surfers, waves are not just natural phenomena—they are a source of excitement, challenge, and adventure.

In conclusion, waves in the Atlantic Ocean are truly amazing. From the powerful swells created by distant storms to the towering rogue waves that appear unexpectedly, the Atlantic is full of incredible wave phenomena. Waves play a crucial role in shaping the ocean and the coastline, supporting marine ecosystems, and providing opportunities for travel, fishing, and even recreation. They are driven by wind, gravity, and the movement of the Earth, and they connect us to the natural rhythms of the planet. Whether you are watching waves crash on the beach, sailing across the ocean, or riding a wave on a surfboard, the waves of the Atlantic are a reminder of the beauty and power of nature.

Chapter 17: Ancient Legends of the Atlantic Ocean

The Atlantic Ocean, stretching between the Americas, Europe, and Africa, has been a source of mystery and inspiration for countless ancient legends and tales. Its vastness, powerful waves, and seemingly endless horizon have fueled the imagination of people for thousands of years. Long before we had modern ships and scientific explanations, ancient civilizations created fascinating stories to explain the wonders of this mighty ocean. These legends have been passed down through generations, evolving and adapting as new cultures encountered the great Atlantic. From sea monsters and lost civilizations to gods and mysterious islands, the Atlantic Ocean has been at the heart of some of the most captivating ancient legends ever told.

One of the most famous and enduring legends associated with the Atlantic Ocean is the story of the lost city of Atlantis. This tale comes from the ancient Greek philosopher Plato, who wrote about Atlantis around 360 BCE. According to Plato, Atlantis was a powerful and advanced civilization that existed thousands of years before his time. The city was said to be located on a large island in the Atlantic Ocean, beyond the "Pillars of Hercules," which we now know as the Strait of Gibraltar. Atlantis was described as a beautiful and wealthy city, with advanced technology, grand temples, and a highly organized society. However, the Atlanteans became greedy and corrupt, and their civilization fell out of favor with the gods. As punishment, the gods sent earthquakes and floods that caused the entire island to sink into the ocean, disappearing forever beneath the waves.

The legend of Atlantis has captivated people for centuries, and many have searched for evidence of the lost city. Although no definitive proof has been found, the story continues to inspire explorers, writers, and scholars. Some believe that Atlantis was a real place, perhaps an island that was destroyed by a natural disaster. Others think it may have been based on the memory of an ancient civilization, such as the Minoans or the Egyptians. Whether or not Atlantis ever truly existed, the legend serves as a cautionary tale about the dangers of pride and greed, and it remains one of the most enduring myths of the Atlantic Ocean.

But the legend of Atlantis is not the only ancient tale associated with the Atlantic. Many cultures that lived along the shores of the Atlantic had their own stories about the ocean and its mysteries. The ancient Celts, who lived in what is now Ireland, Scotland, and parts of France, believed in a mystical place called the Otherworld, a realm of eternal youth, beauty, and abundance. According to Celtic mythology, the Otherworld could be reached by crossing the sea, and it was often described as lying somewhere in the Atlantic Ocean. Some legends speak of islands where the souls of the dead would go to rest, while others tell of heroes who sailed westward to find these magical lands.

One of the most famous Celtic legends is the story of the Isle of Avalon, which is sometimes associated with the Otherworld. Avalon was said to be a paradise, an island of apple trees where the dead could live in peace and harmony. In the legend of King Arthur, it is said that after Arthur was mortally wounded in battle, he was taken by boat to the Isle of Avalon to heal. The idea of a magical island in the Atlantic, where one could escape the troubles of the world, has captured the imagination of many and has parallels in other cultures' stories as well.

The Vikings, the fearless seafaring people from Scandinavia, also had their own legends about the Atlantic Ocean. For the Vikings, the ocean was both a source of opportunity and danger. They ventured across the North Atlantic, exploring new lands such as Iceland, Greenland, and even North America, which they called Vinland. One of the most interesting Viking legends is the tale of Jörmungandr, the Midgard Serpent. In Norse mythology, Jörmungandr was a giant sea serpent so large that it could wrap itself around the entire world and bite its own tail. The Vikings believed that Jörmungandr lived in the ocean and that when it released its tail, it would signal the beginning of Ragnarök, the end of the world. The story of Jörmungandr reflects the Vikings' deep respect for the power of the ocean and the belief that the sea held both life and death.

In addition to sea monsters like Jörmungandr, many ancient cultures believed in other dangerous creatures that lived in the Atlantic Ocean. Sailors often told tales of giant squids, monstrous whales, and creatures that could drag ships beneath the waves. One of the most famous mythical creatures of the sea is the Kraken, a terrifying sea monster from Scandinavian folklore. The Kraken was said to be a giant octopus or squid that lived off the coast of Norway and Greenland. It was so large that it could wrap its tentacles around entire ships, pulling them down to the ocean floor. The Kraken was feared by sailors for centuries, and stories of encounters with the creature were passed down through generations. While the Kraken was likely inspired by real-life giant squids, which can grow up to 40 feet long, the legends turned this animal into a fearsome monster that continues to appear in popular culture today.

The Atlantic Ocean was also seen as a gateway to unknown lands. Before the Age of Exploration, many people believed that the world ended somewhere in the middle of the Atlantic, beyond which there was nothing but darkness and chaos. Sailors feared sailing too far west, thinking they might fall off the edge of the Earth or be swallowed by sea monsters. In the medieval European imagination, the Atlantic was sometimes called the "Sea of Darkness," because its vast, uncharted waters were full of danger and mystery. Only the bravest explorers dared to venture into the unknown, and many of the early attempts to cross the Atlantic ended in shipwrecks and tragedy.

Despite these fears, the Atlantic also represented hope and discovery. For centuries, people told stories of islands that existed somewhere in the Atlantic Ocean, waiting to be found by daring adventurers. One such island was Hy-Brasil, a mythical island said to lie off the west coast of Ireland. According to legend, Hy-Brasil was shrouded in mist and could only be seen once every seven years. Those who managed to reach the island found it to be a paradise, filled with wealth and happiness. Like Atlantis, Hy-Brasil became a symbol of the mysterious and uncharted territories that lay beyond the known world.

In addition to islands and sea monsters, ancient legends also spoke of gods and deities who ruled the Atlantic Ocean. The ancient Greeks believed that Poseidon, the god of the sea, controlled the waters of the Atlantic. Poseidon was a powerful and temperamental god, known for causing earthquakes and storms when he was angry. Sailors would often pray to Poseidon for safe passage across the ocean, offering sacrifices to appease him. In Roman mythology, Poseidon's counterpart was Neptune, who was also revered as the god of the sea. Like Poseidon, Neptune was believed to have the power to calm or stir the waters of the ocean, and he was often depicted holding a trident, his weapon of choice.

Another interesting legend comes from the indigenous people of the Americas, who lived along the Atlantic coast long before the arrival of European explorers. The Taino people, who lived in the Caribbean, believed in a god of the sea named Juracán, who was responsible for creating the powerful hurricanes that swept across the Atlantic. The Taino believed that Juracán lived in the ocean and that his anger would cause the winds and waves to rise, creating destructive storms. This belief helped the Taino people explain the natural forces that shaped their world, and it reflects the deep connection between the ocean and the weather.

The ancient legends of the Atlantic Ocean reveal how humans have long been fascinated by the sea. Whether through stories of lost cities like Atlantis, mysterious islands like Hy-Brasil, or terrifying creatures like the Kraken, the Atlantic has always been a place of wonder, danger, and adventure. These tales have shaped the way people view the ocean, turning it into a realm of mystery where anything is possible. Even today, as we explore the depths of the Atlantic with modern technology, the ocean still holds secrets waiting to be discovered. The ancient legends remind us that the sea has always been a powerful force in human history, inspiring both fear and awe as people sought to understand the vast, uncharted waters of the Atlantic.

Chapter 18: Atlantic Ocean's Impact on Global Climate

The Atlantic Ocean plays a massive and complex role in shaping the Earth's climate. It's like a giant engine that helps to move heat around the planet, influencing weather patterns, temperatures, and even the amount of rainfall in different regions. This impact is felt not just by the countries that border the Atlantic, but by the entire world. To truly understand how the Atlantic Ocean affects global climate, we need to dive deep into the powerful currents, the vast stretches of water, and the important interactions between the ocean and the atmosphere.

One of the most important ways the Atlantic Ocean influences global climate is through a process known as ocean circulation. The Atlantic is home to a massive system of currents that move water around the globe, much like a conveyor belt. This system is part of what's called the "global ocean conveyor belt" or the thermohaline circulation. The word "thermohaline" comes from "thermo," which means heat, and "haline," which refers to the saltiness of the water. Together, heat and salt are key players in how water moves through the ocean.

In the Atlantic, warm water from the tropics flows northward along the surface of the ocean. As this warm water travels, it carries heat with it, helping to warm up the atmosphere and the coastal regions of places like Europe and North America. This is why places like the United Kingdom and parts of northern Europe have much milder winters than you might expect, considering how far north they are. The warm water of the Atlantic keeps the air above it warmer, which in turn makes the climate in those regions more temperate.

But as the warm water moves north, it gradually cools down. In the far North Atlantic, near Greenland and Iceland, the water becomes very cold and dense. When water gets cold, it becomes heavier and sinks down to the bottom of the ocean. This sinking water then begins to flow southward, deep below the surface. This is one part of the global conveyor belt, where cold, dense water moves deep below the surface of the ocean, carrying cold water toward the southern hemisphere. It's almost like an underwater river, moving in the opposite direction of the warm surface currents.

This movement of water – warm water flowing north and cold water flowing south – is crucial for regulating the Earth's climate. It helps distribute heat across the planet, preventing some regions from becoming too hot while others remain too cold. This balancing act is one of the reasons why the Earth's climate is relatively stable. However, if this circulation were to slow down or stop, it could have dramatic effects on the global climate.

Scientists have been studying how climate change might affect this ocean circulation, particularly in the Atlantic. As the planet warms, glaciers and ice sheets in places like Greenland are melting at a faster rate. This adds a large amount of fresh water to the ocean. Freshwater is less dense than saltwater, so if too much freshwater enters the North Atlantic, it could disrupt the sinking process of the cold water. If the cold water doesn't sink, the whole conveyor belt could slow down, which would affect the movement of heat around the planet.

If the Atlantic circulation were to weaken, one possible consequence could be much colder winters in northern Europe. Without the warm water flowing north, places like the United Kingdom and Scandinavia might experience much harsher and longer winters. On the other hand, some parts of the tropics could become even warmer, as less heat would be carried away by the currents. This imbalance could lead to more extreme weather events, such as stronger hurricanes, heatwaves, and droughts in certain parts of the world.

The Atlantic Ocean also plays a key role in regulating the amount of carbon dioxide in the atmosphere. Carbon dioxide is one of the greenhouse gases that trap heat in the Earth's atmosphere, and the ocean acts like a giant sponge, absorbing a significant amount of the carbon dioxide that we produce. The Atlantic Ocean is particularly important in this process because of its strong circulation patterns. As the cold water sinks in the North Atlantic, it carries with it carbon dioxide that has been absorbed from the atmosphere. This carbon dioxide is then stored deep in the ocean for hundreds or even thousands of years.

However, as the ocean absorbs more and more carbon dioxide, it becomes more acidic. This process, known as ocean acidification, can have harmful effects on marine life, particularly organisms like corals and shellfish that rely on calcium carbonate to build their skeletons and shells. If the ocean becomes too acidic, it can dissolve the calcium carbonate, making it harder for these animals to survive. This is yet another way in which the Atlantic Ocean is connected to the health of the global climate and ecosystems.

In addition to its role in moving heat and carbon dioxide, the Atlantic Ocean also affects global climate through the interaction between the ocean and the atmosphere. The ocean and atmosphere are constantly exchanging heat and moisture, which has a big impact on weather patterns. One of the most well-known examples of this interaction is the Atlantic hurricane season.

Hurricanes are powerful storms that form over warm ocean waters, and the Atlantic Ocean is a major breeding ground for these storms. The warmer the ocean water, the more energy a hurricane can gather, which is why hurricanes tend to be more intense when the sea surface temperatures are higher. As the Atlantic warms due to climate change, we could see more frequent and stronger hurricanes. These storms can have devastating effects, not just on coastal regions but also on inland areas that experience flooding and heavy rainfall.

The warming of the Atlantic is also linked to changes in rainfall patterns around the world. For example, the monsoon rains in West Africa, which are crucial for agriculture and water supply, are influenced by the temperature of the Atlantic Ocean. When the Atlantic is warmer than usual, it can disrupt the normal monsoon patterns, leading to droughts in some areas and floods in others. This shows how interconnected the ocean and climate systems are, and how changes in one part of the world can have ripple effects in other regions.

Another important aspect of the Atlantic Ocean's impact on global climate is its role in the El Niño and La Niña phenomena, which are large-scale climate patterns that occur in the Pacific Ocean but can influence weather around the world, including in the Atlantic. During an El Niño event, the Pacific Ocean becomes warmer than usual, which can disrupt the normal trade winds and weather patterns. This can lead to changes in the Atlantic as well, such as fewer hurricanes or changes in the amount of rainfall in certain regions. La Niña, on the other hand, is the opposite of El Niño and tends to bring cooler conditions to the Pacific, which can have different effects on the Atlantic climate.

The Atlantic Ocean is also responsible for what's known as the North Atlantic Oscillation (NAO), a natural climate pattern that influences weather in the North Atlantic region, including parts of Europe, North America, and the Arctic. The NAO is driven by changes in the atmospheric pressure between the Azores, a group of islands in the Atlantic, and Iceland. When the NAO is in a positive phase, it brings mild and wet winters to northern Europe and cold, dry winters to Greenland and Canada. When it's in a negative phase, the pattern is reversed, with colder, snowier winters in Europe and milder winters in Greenland. This oscillation has a major impact on the weather in these regions and can change from year to year.

Overall, the Atlantic Ocean is like a giant climate regulator, influencing everything from local weather patterns to global temperature balances. Its powerful currents, ability to store carbon, and interactions with the atmosphere make it one of the most important factors in the Earth's climate system. Scientists are continuing to study the Atlantic to better understand how it will respond to climate change and how these changes will affect the rest of the world. The ocean holds many secrets, and unlocking them is key to understanding how we can protect our planet and adapt to a changing climate. As we continue to explore and learn more about the Atlantic, we can better appreciate its crucial role in shaping the world's climate and how much our future depends on its health and stability.

Chapter 19: The Trade Routes of the Atlantic

The Atlantic Ocean has long been a major highway for global trade, connecting continents and cultures across vast distances. From ancient times to the modern era, the Atlantic's trade routes have shaped economies, powered empires, and fostered exchanges of goods, ideas, and even people. These routes crisscross the ocean, linking Europe, Africa, the Americas, and beyond, making the Atlantic one of the busiest and most important oceans for international trade. Understanding the history and significance of these trade routes gives us a glimpse into how interconnected the world has become and how vital the Atlantic is to global commerce.

One of the most famous and historically significant trade routes across the Atlantic is the Triangular Trade, which took place from the 16th to the 19th century. This route connected Europe, Africa, and the Americas in a triangular shape, hence the name. Ships from Europe would set sail with goods like textiles, weapons, and manufactured items. They would travel to the west coast of Africa, where these goods were traded for enslaved people. The ships would then make the treacherous Middle Passage across the Atlantic to the Americas, where the enslaved individuals were sold to work on plantations. The final leg of the triangle involved the transport of raw materials like sugar, cotton, tobacco, and coffee back to Europe. These goods, produced through the forced labor of enslaved Africans, fueled the economies of European countries and their colonies.

The Triangular Trade was not only a dark chapter in human history because of the millions of Africans forcibly taken from their homes and sold into slavery, but it also laid the foundation for the Atlantic as a major trade highway. Ships crossed the ocean regularly, establishing well-worn routes that would continue to evolve over time. Today, many of the same routes used during the Triangular Trade remain key channels for global trade, though the cargo has changed drastically.

After the abolition of the transatlantic slave trade, other forms of commerce continued to dominate the Atlantic trade routes. During the Age of Exploration in the 15th and 16th centuries, European powers like Spain, Portugal, France, and England were eager to find new trade routes to Asia and the Americas. The Atlantic became a crucial link for explorers and merchants seeking to expand their reach. Spanish and Portuguese explorers like Christopher Columbus and Vasco da Gama led the way, opening up new possibilities for trade between Europe and the New World.

With the discovery of the Americas, European nations established colonies in the Caribbean, South America, and North America. These colonies were rich in natural resources like gold, silver, sugar, and spices, which European traders were eager to acquire. The Atlantic Ocean became the primary route for transporting these valuable goods back to Europe. Ships laden with treasure sailed across the ocean, returning to Europe with wealth that would help fund the growth of cities, the construction of grand palaces, and the expansion of European empires.

In the 17th and 18th centuries, the Atlantic trade routes saw the rise of the sugar and tobacco industries, both of which relied heavily on the Atlantic for transporting goods. Sugar plantations in the Caribbean produced vast quantities of sugar, which was a highly sought-after commodity in Europe. Similarly, tobacco grown in the American colonies became a popular product that European consumers couldn't get enough of. Ships carrying barrels of sugar and tobacco regularly made the journey across the Atlantic, creating a booming transatlantic trade that brought wealth to merchants and plantation owners.

In addition to raw materials, European settlers in the Americas needed manufactured goods from Europe. Ships crossing the Atlantic in the other direction were often filled with tools, clothing, and other necessities for the growing colonies. This two-way trade established strong economic ties between Europe and its colonies, with the Atlantic Ocean serving as the lifeline for both sides. Without the steady flow of goods across the Atlantic, the colonies might not have been able to survive or thrive as they did.

As the world moved into the 19th century and the Industrial Revolution began, the importance of the Atlantic trade routes only grew. Factories in Europe and the northeastern United States needed raw materials like cotton and coal to power their machines. The southern United States became a major exporter of cotton, which was shipped across the Atlantic to European factories where it was turned into textiles. The demand for cotton, in particular, led to the development of some of the most important and well-used trade routes in the Atlantic.

During this time, the introduction of steamships revolutionized transatlantic trade. Unlike the sailing ships of earlier centuries, steamships were faster and more reliable, making it easier to transport goods over long distances. Steamships could also carry more cargo than sailing ships, which meant that more goods could be transported across the Atlantic in shorter amounts of time. This innovation dramatically increased the volume of trade between Europe, the Americas, and other parts of the world, solidifying the Atlantic's position as a vital artery for global commerce.

One of the most famous steamship routes across the Atlantic was the transatlantic passenger service, which connected Europe and the United States. These routes not only carried goods but also people—immigrants seeking new lives in the Americas, tourists, and businessmen traveling for trade. New York City and Liverpool in England became major ports for this transatlantic traffic, and the ships that sailed these routes became iconic symbols of the era. The Titanic, perhaps the most famous steamship of all, was part of this network of ships crossing the Atlantic.

In the 20th century, the Atlantic trade routes played a key role during both World War I and World War II. The Atlantic was a critical theater of naval operations, as the Allies and Axis powers fought to control the shipping lanes that supplied goods, weapons, and troops. The famous Battle of the Atlantic during World War II was a prolonged struggle for control of these crucial trade routes. German submarines, or U-boats, attempted to disrupt the Allied supply lines by sinking merchant ships carrying essential supplies from North America to Europe. The Allies, in turn, used convoys and naval escorts to protect these ships, ensuring that the vital flow of goods continued across the Atlantic.

Today, the Atlantic Ocean remains one of the busiest and most important trade routes in the world. Modern container ships, some of the largest vessels ever built, crisscross the Atlantic daily, carrying everything from electronics and automobiles to food and clothing. The Atlantic connects some of the world's largest economies, including the United States, Canada, the European Union, and Brazil. Ports along the Atlantic coasts of North America, South America, Europe, and Africa serve as hubs for the global economy, with ships constantly loading and unloading goods.

One of the most important modern trade routes in the Atlantic is the route between the United States and Europe. This route handles a significant portion of global trade, with millions of tons of goods being transported between these two economic powerhouses every year. From consumer goods like clothing and electronics to industrial products like machinery and chemicals, the Atlantic serves as the main conduit for trade between the U.S. and the European Union, which are each other's largest trading partners.

In addition to the U.S.-Europe route, the Atlantic is also home to important trade routes that connect North America with South America and Europe with Africa. These routes are crucial for the movement of agricultural products, energy resources, and raw materials that fuel industries around the world. For example, Brazil, a major exporter of coffee, sugar, and soybeans, relies on Atlantic trade routes to ship its products to markets in Europe and North America. Similarly, countries in West Africa export goods like cocoa, rubber, and oil to the rest of the world through the Atlantic.

The Atlantic trade routes are also vital for the energy sector. Large oil tankers travel across the Atlantic carrying crude oil from producers in South America, West Africa, and the Middle East to refineries in North America and Europe. Natural gas, coal, and other energy resources are also transported across the Atlantic, making the ocean an essential link in the global energy supply chain.

Looking to the future, the Atlantic trade routes are expected to remain critical for global commerce. However, challenges such as climate change, overfishing, and pollution could affect the health of the Atlantic and the industries that depend on it. As shipping and trade continue to grow, protecting the Atlantic's ecosystems and ensuring sustainable practices will be crucial for preserving this important global resource.

In conclusion, the trade routes of the Atlantic Ocean have been a driving force in the world's economic development for centuries. From the dark days of the Triangular Trade to the bustling container ports of today, the Atlantic has connected nations, facilitated the exchange of goods, and played a central role in shaping the global economy. Its currents, winds, and vast open waters have made it an essential artery for international trade, and its impact on the world's economic systems will continue to be felt for generations to come.

Chapter 20: Life Along the Atlantic Coastlines

Life along the Atlantic coastlines is incredibly diverse, vibrant, and deeply connected to the ocean. Stretching from the icy shores of northern Canada to the warm beaches of South America and Africa, the Atlantic Ocean touches the lives of millions of people and a vast range of ecosystems. The coastlines of the Atlantic are not only home to stunning natural beauty but also bustling cities, charming fishing villages, and unique wildlife. For thousands of years, people have lived along these coastlines, depending on the ocean for food, transportation, and commerce. The Atlantic coastlines are places of adventure, survival, history, and constant change, shaped by both human activity and the natural forces of the ocean.

One of the most striking features of life along the Atlantic coastlines is the sheer diversity of environments. On the northern edges of the Atlantic, you'll find cold, rugged landscapes with cliffs, fjords, and forests. The coastlines of places like Canada, Iceland, and Norway are often rocky and dramatic, where the land meets the powerful waves of the cold Atlantic. These areas are home to hardy animals like puffins, seals, and whales, as well as forests of kelp and other cold-water sea plants. Despite the harsh conditions, people have lived here for centuries, with fishing being one of the main industries. In places like Newfoundland and the Faroe Islands, entire communities have built their lives around catching fish like cod, herring, and mackerel. The cold, nutrient-rich waters of the North Atlantic support an abundance of marine life, making fishing a vital part of the culture and economy.

Moving south along the Atlantic, the coastline changes dramatically. As you enter the more temperate regions of Europe and North America, the landscape softens into sandy beaches, salt marshes, and estuaries. These coastal areas are home to bustling cities like New

York, Lisbon, and Buenos Aires, where millions of people live and work. The ocean plays a central role in the economies of these regions, from shipping and tourism to fishing and aquaculture. The ports along the Atlantic coast are some of the busiest in the world, with cargo ships bringing in goods from all corners of the globe. The cities themselves are deeply connected to the sea, with harbors, beaches, and promenades being important places for both business and leisure.

One of the most unique features of the Atlantic coastline is the presence of vast wetlands and marshes. These ecosystems, found in places like the eastern United States, the Caribbean, and parts of West Africa, are incredibly rich in biodiversity. Salt marshes, mangrove forests, and coastal wetlands provide critical habitats for fish, birds, and other wildlife. In the United States, for example, the Atlantic coastal plain is home to species like blue crabs, shrimp, and the famous horseshoe crab, which comes ashore to lay its eggs every year. These wetlands also serve as natural buffers against storms and flooding, absorbing water and reducing the impact of hurricanes and other natural disasters. In places like Florida, the Everglades and other coastal wetlands are important not only for wildlife but also for the people who rely on them for fishing, farming, and tourism.

Farther south, in the tropical regions of the Atlantic, the coastline is lined with coral reefs, palm trees, and turquoise waters. In the Caribbean, the coastlines are dotted with islands, each with its own unique blend of cultures, traditions, and ecosystems. The warm waters of the tropical Atlantic support coral reefs, which are home to thousands of species of fish, sea turtles, and other marine creatures. These reefs are not only important for biodiversity but also for the people who live along the coast. Fishing, tourism, and recreation all depend on the health of these coral ecosystems. In places like the Bahamas, the Dominican Republic, and the Yucatan Peninsula, the tourism industry is a major part of life, with visitors coming from around the world to enjoy the warm weather, clear waters, and stunning beaches. Snorkeling, diving, and fishing are popular activities, and many people make their livelihoods by working in the tourism industry.

However, life along the Atlantic coastlines is not without its challenges. Coastal areas are often vulnerable to natural disasters, such as hurricanes, floods, and rising sea levels. In places like Florida and the Gulf Coast of the United States, hurricanes can cause immense destruction, damaging homes, infrastructure, and ecosystems. In the Caribbean, hurricanes are a constant threat during the storm season, with powerful winds and waves battering the islands and causing flooding. In West Africa, rising sea levels are slowly eroding the coastline, threatening communities and farmland. Coastal erosion is also a problem in many other parts of the Atlantic, as the waves and tides gradually wear away the land, reshaping the coastline over time.

Another challenge facing life along the Atlantic coastlines is the impact of human activity on the environment. Pollution from cities, industries, and agriculture often finds its way into the ocean, affecting the health of coastal ecosystems. In many places, plastic waste, oil spills, and chemical runoff have harmed marine life, from fish and birds to coral reefs and seagrass beds. Overfishing is another major issue, with some fish populations being depleted by commercial fishing operations. In response to these challenges, many coastal communities and governments have taken steps to protect the Atlantic coastline. Marine protected areas, sustainable fishing practices, and efforts to reduce pollution are all part of the movement to preserve the health of the ocean and its ecosystems.

Despite these challenges, life along the Atlantic coastlines remains vibrant and full of possibility. The people who live here have always been deeply connected to the ocean, and that connection continues to shape their lives today. Coastal communities often have a rich maritime culture, with traditions, music, and festivals that celebrate the sea. In places like Cape Cod in the United States, fishing villages in Portugal, and the coast of Senegal, the rhythm of life is still tied to the tides, the seasons, and the movements of the fish. Festivals like the Blessing of the Fleet, which takes place in many coastal towns, are a way for people to honor their connection to the ocean and give thanks for its bounty.

For children growing up along the Atlantic coast, the ocean is a place of adventure and learning. Whether it's exploring tide pools, swimming in the waves, or sailing on a boat, the coast offers endless opportunities to experience the wonders of the natural world. Many schools and organizations offer programs that teach kids about marine biology, conservation, and the importance of protecting the ocean. In some places, kids participate in beach cleanups, helping to remove plastic and other debris from the shorelines. These activities not only teach young people about the ocean but also instill a sense of responsibility for taking care of the environment.

In addition to the people who live and work along the coast, the Atlantic coastlines are home to countless species of animals. Seabirds like gulls, pelicans, and albatrosses soar over the waves, while dolphins, seals, and whales swim in the waters below. Sea turtles nest on the sandy beaches, while crabs and other creatures scuttle along the shore. The estuaries and wetlands are teeming with life, providing breeding grounds for fish, shrimp, and other marine animals. Coral reefs, seagrass beds, and mangrove forests serve as nurseries for young fish and protect the coastline from erosion and storms. The Atlantic's rich biodiversity is a reminder of how important the ocean is for the health of the planet and all its inhabitants.

Life along the Atlantic coastlines is a fascinating blend of natural beauty, human history, and ecological diversity. From the cold waters of the North Atlantic to the warm, sunny beaches of the Caribbean, the coastlines offer a glimpse into how people and nature coexist in a constantly changing environment. Whether it's a fishing village in Iceland, a bustling port city in Brazil, or a tropical island in the Caribbean, the Atlantic's coastlines are full of stories waiting to be discovered. The ocean has shaped the way people live, work, and play, and it continues to be a source of wonder and inspiration for everyone who calls the coast their home.

Epilogue

And so, we've reached the end of our incredible journey across the Atlantic Ocean! From exploring its deep, mysterious waters to learning about the creatures that call it home, we've uncovered many of the ocean's amazing secrets. The Atlantic has shown us its powerful tides, stormy weather, and how important it is for the balance of life on Earth. We've even explored the legends and stories that have been passed down through generations, all centered around this mighty ocean.

But the adventure doesn't end here! The Atlantic Ocean is constantly changing, and there's always more to discover. Whether it's new species being found in the deep, scientific breakthroughs about ocean currents, or efforts to protect this incredible environment, the Atlantic's story is still being written—and you can be a part of it!

As you close this book, remember that the ocean is full of wonder and mystery. The more we learn about it, the more we can appreciate its beauty and the role it plays in our world. Maybe one day, you'll be the one making exciting discoveries about the Atlantic Ocean!

So, keep exploring, stay curious, and never stop learning about the amazing planet we call home. The Atlantic Ocean will always be there, waiting for the next great adventure.

The End.

Milton Keynes UK
Ingram Content Group UK Ltd.
UKHW042239011124
450424UK00001BA/93